Lilla Bek sees energies nor~~mally invisible to the~~
naked eye. Following a we~~ek~~
with exercise, prayer an~~d m~~
began to realise her psy~~chic power~~
became acutely aware of so~~unds and was able to~~
see minute structures and en~~ergy fields that had~~
previously been invisible to her.

This book is intended to provide you with a
bridge to a more developed sense of
awareness. There are exercises at the end of
each section which will help you relax, breathe
and visualise better. It will also help anybody
who may be experiencing symptoms that they
are unable to control, to understand what is
happening so that their energy can be ordered
and perhaps begin to be aware of the reason
and purpose of being on earth.

TO THE LIGHT

Lilla Bek
with
Philippa Pullar

UNWIN PAPERBACKS
London · Boston · Sydney

First published by Unwin Paperbacks 1985.

UNWIN ® PAPERBACKS
40 Museum Street, London WC1A 1LU, UK

Unwin Paperbacks
Park Lane, Hemel Hempstead, Herts HP2 4TE, UK

George Allen & Unwin Australia Pty Ltd
8 Napier Street, North Sydney, NSW 2060, Australia

Unwin Paperbacks with the
Port Nicholson Press
PO Box 11–838 Wellington, New Zealand

British Library Cataloguing in Publication Data

Bek, Lilla
  To the light.
  1. Psychical research
  I. Title   II. Pullar, Philippa
  133.8   BF1031
  ISBN 0–04–131026–8

Set in 11 on 12 point Imprint by Phoenix Photosetting, Chatham
and printed in Great Britain by
The Guernsey Press Co Ltd, Guernsey, Channel Islands.

Contents

List of Illustrations

Preface

Fourteen years ago, Lilla began seeing energies that are normally invisible to the human eye. Up to then her life had been uncomplicated, happily taken up with her family, animals and hobbies. She painted, skated, played tennis, embroidered, knitted the most beautiful clothes, and then took up karate and yoga. Before going further, I would like to say that it is not my intention here to present Lilla as a cosy housewife sitting knitting by her fireside. There was certainly nothing weird, nothing particularly extraordinary about her; yet the important thing is that she possessed the qualities essential to success in any project: namely, enthusiasm for anything she set out to do, the ability to concentrate on it and the necessary stamina to follow it through. It was at Glastonbury, during an intensive week of yoga, seven years after she had begun practising it, that something happened which led to the opening up of her psychic gifts. First of all, Glastonbury is famous for being one of the most powerful places in England. Secondly, the convent where the group were staying was especially highly charged, not only by the fact of its location, close to the ruins, but also by the prayers of the nuns.

The entire week was devoted to yogic activities – exercise, prayer and meditation – and for Lilla the effect of these was increased even further by the fact that she was then subsisting only on glucose. Such plainness had not been her intention, but, whether because of an infection she had caught or because of the cathartic properties of the convent diet, any food she took passed straight through her system, obliging her to go on what was effectively a fast. This combination of cleansed body, purified mind and highly charged environment led her to have the sort of mystical experience that in India is traditionally known as the awakening of the Kundalini, when that force which lies coiled like a snake at the base of the spine rises explosively into the brain and in doing so transforms the consciousness of the individual.[1] This energy seized her, pushing her up the bed she was lying in three times, so violently, so convulsively that she thought she was having an epileptic fit. Yet the feeling was so beautiful and so unforgettable that, she says, anyone who has experienced anything like it cannot help but be driven into finding a way of giving it to others.

After this, Lilla found she was able to see minute structures and energy fields that had previously been invisible to her. She could hear the pulse beating in the atom, hear too the sounds of stones, trees and plants. She was, however, not pleased. This new sense was initially not merely inconvenient but frightening, whereas before everything had been so straightforward. A great many interests had occupied her both mentally and physically; indeed, the amount of energy she invested in her activities had become something of a joke in her family. Her spirit also had been well provided for – as a Roman Catholic she was, she says, deeply religious – yet this new gift now went against everything in which she believed.

Sometimes it was as though she were unable to close her eyes: no matter how firmly she shut them or how dark it was she could still see quite clearly through her eyelids. All kinds of odd things would happen. A friend might telephone, and Lilla would see that person at the other end of the line: on one occasion, a girl was sitting there dressed only in the underwear they had recently bought together on a shopping spree! Once Lilla was late and frantically preparing for a dinner party when she suddenly saw the guests, ready and approaching rapidly; sure enough, they arrived at her door soon afterwards, long before she had finished. There was another appalling time, at the British Museum, when all the cabinets suddenly came to life: each exhibit seemed to contain a small screen upon which its history unwound. Try as she might, she was unable to switch this off until she discovered an archaeological lecture tour in progress: as soon as she joined this group its intellectual energy had the effect of closing down her vision.

Lilla is not a person to be easily intimidated. She decided to conduct some research for the purpose of establishing whether the things she was seeing were authentic or whether she was only imagining them. And she applied herself to the task in her usual energetic way. She carried out mental diagnoses, tuned into and read hundreds of signatures and, in order to study changes in mental awareness, did night duty in a psychiatric hospital. She spent many hours in deep concentration, focusing on objects and their energy fields. She kept checking and rechecking, comparing her observations with the findings of Kirlian photography. It was hard, time-consuming work: half of her wished it would all go away and that her research would prove nothing while the other half found the whole thing fascinating. Again and again she would return to a case or an article, working with subjects of which she had no previous knowledge, observing and finding her observations verified by the findings of others, until eventually she was able to establish a real inner sense of knowing whether or not she was accurate.

Gradually her observations began to yield a number of interesting results. She discovered that by arousing her energies or stimulating certain parts of her body – for example, by raising her palate and altering the position of her ears – she could bring about a change in her consciousness. She found she could alter her brainwaves through meditation and that this was easier to achieve at night than during the day; that she could empty her mind and reprogramme it, as it were; and that it was possible to unlock impressions from subconscious levels and remove them, to feed in data and also receive new information. She found that breaking through for the first time was difficult, requiring concentration, perseverance and confidence, and that sounds and symbols – ranging from music to mantras, deities to glasses of water – could be helpful signals to the psyche, techniques for triggering off the necessary transformation. After a while she grew able to use her body like an instrument; but all instruments need a constant current of energy in order to function efficiently, and Lilla was no exception. It was only possible, she discovered, to produce and maintain a current of energy over a certain space of time; when it ran down, she had to relax and recharge it. Little by little, she became capable of doing all kinds of extraordinary things that interested her very much. Sometimes she worked on research projects and courses involving the use of special monitoring equipment, and after sitting for many hours adjusting her energies she found she could recognise the type of brainwave she was employing.

Any action depends for its effectiveness on the strength of its motivation, and psychic work depends for its success on precision and direction; in other words, it is essential to be absolutely positive. If at any time the result did not seem clear enough, Lilla would complain and send it back 'upstairs', demanding something clearer. Dealing with the invisible is a bit like *Alice in Wonderland*: anything can be blown up and examined as though under a microscope, but if you 'think small' and are timid, nothing will happen. Lilla found that, first and foremost, it was vital to have a very definite idea of what she was doing. If, for instance, she were embarking on historical research, there was no question of her sitting back and taking pot luck, just as there would be no question of picking up books at random if one were trying to write, say, a paper on Anglo-Saxon archaeology in the Thames estuary. She would specify which aspect of her subject, which civilisation, she wanted to contact: medicine in Lemuria, perhaps; crystals in Atlantis; farming in ancient Crete; gardening in Greece.

To give an example: one of Lilla's projects was a study of the training of dancing girls in Pharaonic Egyptian temples; she has established that in one of her previous lives she herself used to train dancers. She has succeeded in restoring this knowledge and now teaches some of the sacred temple dances on her courses. In the case of a large temple, some 500 girls would initially be selected for training – and the story as it unfolds is faintly reminiscent of Agatha Christie's *Ten Little Niggers*. They each had to have a good figure and appearance, to have had experience of dance in past lives and to be of approximately the same height as the others. During the first stage they were given no work and no training; they simply remained in the temple under observation, and one by one the lazy and the frivolous were weeded out. The next step was different: here the girls were submitted to a strict regime of yogic exercise, concentration, meditation and practical work. Any who tired easily or complained were now dismissed. By the end of this stage possibly 200 of the original number remained. From then on the training became more difficult, incorporating the manipulation of brainwaves, the monitoring of awareness and the establishing of telepathic, astral and mental projection. The girls had, ultimately, to become the music and the movement; yet they also had to project themselves in such a way that they could include and take over the audience. Every movement of the hands, fingers, legs and toes had to be registered and the different ways in which these influenced the body and the consciousness recorded. Probably only fifty of the original 500 would make it to the end.

In time, Lilla's observations began to supply the answers to all sorts of questions: why, for example, epileptics have energies in their feet that come and go and why before a person suffers a stroke certain of his energies disappear altogether. She saw that as far as disease is concerned it is when energies move either too fast or too slow that problems occur, so that while illness can take many forms it is always rooted either in the slowing down or speeding up of energy fields. She saw, too, that many mental patients possess psychic gifts which they can neither control nor understand; that overcharged energy can create visions and lead one to hear voices, even music. The composer Rachmaninov suffered from this towards the end of his life, being unable to switch off the music that seemed to be playing in his ears. 'Who is it who keeps playing?' he asked his wife. 'Why do they keep on playing?' When she assured him that no one was playing, he understood: 'Aah! . . . that means it's playing in my head.'[2] The point here is that clairvoyance and clairaudience should be accepted and understood as a stage in evolution rather than dismissed as something strange.

Finally, a brief note on how this book came to be written. The body of information was dictated directly on to tape by Lilla, and it was my job to shape this material into a narrative and, where necessary, to back it up with references and historical material.

Philippa Pullar

Introduction

The invisible forces of the universe have long been worshipped in the name of religion and their secrets closely guarded. The result has been that all through history innumerable people have used esoteric knowledge as a means for personal gain, as a tool for controlling and changing the minds of others in order to amass power. There have, of course, been holy and sincere teachers, yet there have also been plenty of ambitious spiritual materialists more interested in appropriating power for their own use. The history of man and his civilisation could well be seen as an exercise in the abuse of power, a struggle to monopolise the sources of energy.

Before going any further it is necessary to draw up a simple historical background so as to trace the patterns against which we are now standing. Fundamental to supplies of energy on this planet is land. In the beginning, the earth supplied the food to feed the men to produce the power to defend and fight for more land, which in turn produced more food and therefore more power – which sounds like a nursery rhyme. The lust for more and more land, more and more power, lies at the heart of our turbulent, war-torn centuries. Changes led to the Industrial Revolution, and man found the means to harness fossil fuels and convert them into energy, thereby replacing his own power. Nowadays, instead of exercising his own power, man is dependent on these fuels for his urban industrial existence while being simultaneously haunted by the fear that sooner rather than later such resources will be exhausted. Our present age is gripped by the spirit of economics; economists are today's high priests, and economic growth the highest of values. Man is thus reduced to the level of a consuming machine and nature viewed as something to be exploited and dominated. As Jung[3] points out, man has acquired a certain amount of will-power which he can apply where he pleases. He can do his work efficiently without recourse to chanting and drumming, he can even dispense with a daily prayer for divine aid. Yet in order to sustain his creed, contemporary man pays the price in a remarkable lack of introspection. He is blind to the fact that for all his rationality and efficiency he is possessed by 'powers' that are beyond his control: his gods and demons merely have new names. They keep him on the run with restlessness, vague apprehensions, psychological complications and an insatiable need for food, sex, pills, alcohol and tobacco: 'Modern man does not understand how much his "rationalism" has put him at the mercy of the psychic underworld. He has freed himself from superstition but in the process has lost his spiritual values to a positively dangerous degree.'[4]

Against the advances of materialism the orthodox Church has shown a remarkable inadequacy, its members appearing to withdraw from the world to argue among themselves about such matters as birth control and infallibility of the Pope. It is the Establishment's inability to deal with the ravages of economics, pollution and deterioration caused by modern agricultural practices (to say nothing of orthodox medicine) that has led, on the one hand, to the springing up of nonconformist holistic and conservation movements and, on the other, to a departure towards the mysticism and the more inspiring cultures of the East. Aside from this, Western man finds himself isolated inside his body, estranged from nature and his fellow human beings, existing in a synthetic society which is split into different nations, races, religions and political groups, and identifying himself with his mind in accordance with the Cartesian principle, 'I think; therefore I am.' He oscillates between a number of opposites: East versus West, black versus white, good versus evil, left versus right, intellect versus intuition. One of the principal polarities in life is that which exists between male and female. Western society traditionally favours the former at the expense of the latter. The result is overemphasis on the masculine aspects of human nature – rationality, competition, aggressiveness – as against the female, mystical, intuitive, occult or psychic side. Nowhere is this polarity more evident than in the divide that exists between science and religion. In spite of the breakthrough made by scientists at the beginning of this century, when the quantum theory revealed the basic oneness of the universe, and in spite of the many recent discoveries which we shall touch on later, science and religion appear – to the layman at least – to be as far apart as they ever were. The only acceptable guide for the scientific mind is logical conclusion derived from experiments which makes the 'secret', the 'sacred', seem like nonsense. One of the deepest underlying factors in the breach is perhaps the tradition of secrecy that has shrouded religion ever since the beginning of time. This comes in direct opposition to the spirit of science, which sets out to penetrate the unknowable and to make knowledge as clear and as available as possible. This is the theory; yet in practice, quite apart from that research which for various reasons is carried out in the utmost secrecy, most scientific knowledge is, by nature of its complicated character, unavailable to the majority.

There is an irony here. In the past, knowledge was reserved for the temple élite, that select body of gifted men who held the keys to understanding. Although the sages endeavoured to hand on to posterity revelations of the spirit, these were always disguised in the form of parables, legends and sacred texts whose real essence was evident only to the initiated. In other words, the ancients were not democratic with knowledge. To the uninitiated they provided only a minimal amount of useful teaching. These days we are in more or less the same situation, with few of us capable of understanding the themes of modern science. This means that knowledge of science is in the hands of a restricted élite – a new aristocracy of power.

This brings us to the second source of energy on our planet, which is the cosmos: cosmic energy, in other words. Anyone who has the ability to tap energies issuing from the earth or the cosmos and manipulate them is capable of wielding great power over others. The ancient schools of initiation, whose role was precisely that of teaching neophytes how to acquire such ability, were veiled in secrecy. Initiations into the mysteries were often painful and terrifying ordeals, and the penalty for revealing knowledge was death.

These days one result of scientific development is that most of us are able to harness certain invisible forces daily and with very little effort. Providing we can pay our bills, we can turn on our electric lighting, heating, radio, microwave oven and television whenever we please, and given that our equipment is properly earthed it is unlikely to kill us. Experts are able to go further, employing radar, sonar and X-rays: for instance, they can use sound waves to kill bacteria, to give a fine texture to paint, to make peanut butter and mayonnaise, to measure the ocean and to clean watches and clocks. Yet such forces are only a few in the huge sea of invisible energies that surround us. There are many more that, through lack of knowledge, remain inaccessible to us. And, despite the development of orthodox medicine, there are also great gaps in an understanding of the energies in the human body; indeed, if questioned about the nature of his patient's energy, a Western doctor might even go so far as to say that such a thing does not exist. To put it another way, the oriental doctor considers the energies of his patient as something primary and real whose deficiency causes, secondarily, disease. The Western physician thinks of the chemistry of the body as being of primary importance and only secondarily as affecting energy, and he often excludes his patient's feelings altogether. Both, however, would agree that man uses only a small area of his brain: 3–4 per cent a lecturer during a mind-control course posited recently, going on to add that Einstein himself only used 10 per cent. Whatever the statistic, it is clear that man employs only a tiny portion of his brain: he has yet to penetrate the rest. In short, many of life's mysteries appear to be as mysterious as ever, and there are plenty of people in whose interest it is to keep it that way. Religion, albeit not of the orthodox Christian variety, is one of the boom industries of the second half of the twentieth century, along with alcohol, tobacco and medical drugs. Every year the pundits of the East draw considerable numbers of Westerners; this in spite of the fact that every so often the more notorious gurus and cults turn up in the press, their names splashed across the headlines in connection with sex, drugs, property, kidnapping or some such scandal. Nevertheless, Eastern teachings, inclining as they do towards the intuitive right side of the brain, towards the unity of all things and of all men, continue to attract many who, frustrated by our rational left-brained Western society, hurry away to adopt exotic names, clothes and customs.

Meanwhile, back in the materialist West, cashing in on the boom of spiritual shopping, there is an epidemic of books and teachers. Every sort of meditation and exercise technique is on offer for the opening up of consciousness, yet nowhere is it explained how changes can occur in the body or how difficulties may be experienced when vibratory rates alter. Most teachers are still traditional in their approach, failing, in other words, to explain either their teachings or their exercises. To all intents and purposes they make themselves into gods: essential to the exercise, the meditation, and above all to the student himself. Yet the teacher's role is to instruct the student in the best method of practising the technique for himself, to inspire him to experiment and, in effect, to become a scientist and use his body as a laboratory. The teacher needs to remove himself from the exercise: just as the student should not become addicted to placebos – to drugs, alcohol or cigarettes – neither should he become addicted to his instructor. The highest schools of ancient teaching forbade worship of the teacher: masters did not get their faces depicted on ornaments to be worn around their disciples' necks, or used as a focus of meditation as is so often the case nowadays; nor did these schools require their disciples to adopt modes of dress, names and customs foreign to their own culture. There were none of the trappings which today are used for what amounts to the propagation of idolatry. Of course, there are holy and sincere teachers to be found, and many disciples do return from their gurus strengthened, uplifted and inspired; but there are also plenty of psychic gangsters at large and no doubt some seekers return from ashrams and communes disturbed physically, mentally and spiritually. There is an essential distinction to be made between submitting to a guru and being enslaved by him. Some teachers are powerful and seductive, and to be in the company of such beings may be a ravishing experience: one can receive from them all kinds of effects and sensations. But what happens is that the guru can become a drug, that is to say an addiction. What we are really seeing in such teachers is that original need to amass power, to amass the energy of worshippers.

The role of the East should be to illuminate the spark that lies within us and make us remember that here in the West we too have a right side of the brain and many gifts to develop. It is not really intended that we should adopt oriental ways and customs, just as it is not intended that we should get 'hooked' on other people. We have to develop our own intuition and sensitivity, our own spiritual environment – one that is suited to our climate and will enable us, in our turn, to develop ourselves. In order to do this we need to have a clear explanation of what is happening so as to be able to understand and control our energies and make appropriate choices. If we learn what a particular exercise or technique is doing we might decide against continuing with that one and try another: if, for example, a person is already oversensitive it may not be advisable for him to pursue a technique which teaches him to become more sensitive still. One of the main lessons drummed into Lilla by her own teacher (who, it should be said, prefers to remain anonymous) is that the pupil *must* see and feel for himself: a human being is not a puppet to be programmed by others. Again and again the question was raised: 'What would *you* do now?' Thus she had to work out the mechanics and techniques directly through her own experience, to study exactly what these were doing and how they were affecting her.

Not even the best teachers can supply us with higher consciousness or fill us with knowledge; what we receive depends on our state of readiness and receptivity, on our ability to understand, on our own faculties. A guru is really a mirror: no matter how good his meditation, no matter how wise his words, he cannot change anything, for only we can change ourselves. The most effective instruction is that which leads us to put our problems clearly to ourselves so that we are able to find the answers in meditation.

At the end of each section in this book, practical exercises are given to help you to relax, breathe and visualise better and to develop your sense of awareness. Their object is for you to be creative. These exercises are suggestions for you to expand and develop, to use in the way that is best for you. You may feel, for example, that it would be appropriate for you to make tapes of the visualisation exercises so that you can follow them in meditation. For more detailed yoga exercises dealing with each centre, see *What Colour Are You?* by Lilla Bek and Annie Wilson.[5]

Whatever you do it is essential for you to understand the whole of it. You should know what you are doing, why you are doing it, what can go wrong and how to correct the errors. To put it metaphorically, let us suppose you are living on the bank of a river. You are unable to swim, and every time you need to cross to the opposite bank you have to walk several miles to a toll bridge. If somebody provided you with the rudiments of swimming or bridge construction, you would be able to learn either how to swim across or build your own bridge. This book is a means of helping you to make your own bridge. It is also intended to help anybody who may be experiencing symptoms they are unable to control, to understand what is happening so that their energy can be ordered and perhaps begin to be aware of the reason and purpose of being on earth.

CHAPTER ONE
The System

The purpose of life is to learn to control energy in order that, ultimately, we may transform matter. On this, or rather on the first part of this statement, science and religion are known to agree. We know that economists dream of possessing unlimited powers through harnessing the treasures of the earth. In a sense, there is a grain of truth here: there really is no limit to what can be created through the energies of this planet. Yet the answer does not lie in monopolising the sources of such energies and squandering our resources but in establishing the human body as a high-voltage transformer. Human beings have the potential to transform energy, transmute negativity and create light. 'I see man as a ball of lightning,' says the Russian scientist, Viktor Inyushin. 'A living organism is nothing but a giant liquid crystal; a semiconductor composed of an intricate system of conductors of various stages of conductability.'[6] This view is not common; the physical body is not usually recognised as an electrical circuit.

Nevertheless, a human being has the potential to harness energy from everything on this planet: water, air, earth, animals, minerals, stones, trees and flowers.[7] Hillsides of gorse in full bloom possess an especially vigorous energy. There is a widespread legend, perpetuated by Oscar Wilde, that when the celebrated botanist, Linnaeus, first saw that plant he fell to his knees and gave thanks to God for the 'lovely yellow flowers'. Once we are able to gather, channel and focus energies completely we have access to other lives and dimensions; a person's name has only to be mentioned and we know his whole history, and there are many more things besides, as we shall see. But first, we have to know what we are doing. If we try to understand the idea of transformation we must recognise that we are talking about vibra-

1

tions, light and energy and thinking about the quality and degree of light we can draw into our bodies. Perhaps the most essential thing of all is to question our motives for exploring these realms in the first place. Do we, too, want to amass power? Or are we dabbling for fun, for kicks? Unless our motives are correct we will end up overcharging our systems and burning out our circuits, for these energies are explosive and, like all explosives, highly dangerous. Rules and regulations for safety exist, and all kingdoms, from the animal, vegetable and mineral to the higher dimensions, have particular vibratory rates to which we must accommodate.

Most people's bodies consume excessive energy because they are out of alignment, wrongly fed, overworked, under-exercised or incompletely oxygenated. All religions, yogas, cults and martial arts are, in essence, systems for learning to use the body for harnessing energies; for learning to gather and focus energies rather than dissipate them; for transmuting them in order to raise the consciousness. Every religion talks about the further use of energy, but some are more specific than others in their instruction, using the whole of their bodies to express the energy. Tibetan, Hindu and Buddhist teachings are among those which speak of a second nervous system, an electrical circuit that can be quickened through the performance of various exercises.

The ancient Egyptians, too, taught that the vital organs are transformers for the nervous flux in order that a higher state of consciousness transcending material forms might be awakened.[8] The temple in Egypt (as indeed, elsewhere, such as India, ancient Greece and during the Christian Gothic period in Europe) was a book that revealed an esoteric teaching. Still more, it was the pinnacle of a collective life whereby psycho-spiritual growth was wedded to a precise intellectual discipline: a type of education which was directed towards the embodiment of spiritual knowledge. The point of initiation was one of practicality: to select those individuals who had either developed or were capable of developing the necessary understanding and could be trusted not to misuse the knowledge revealed to them. It was a protection against the abuse of power.

Initiates would make use of all possible facilities for opening consciousness and reaching higher vibratory rates. Drugs were frequently resorted to in order to give the initiate a glimpse of the state towards which he was working: once he had seen it he had to proceed under his own steam, maintaining discipline in order to get there without external aid. Initiation was often difficult and painful, and life in the temples rigorous; yet these were secure and supportive establishments, the whole idea of the temple being that the outer space should be protected so that the initiate might safely concentrate on the inner space. The concept of inner and outer space is an interesting one. Different races and cultures have correspondingly different approaches to space. Many oriental civilisations, together with the Red Indians of North America, have always considered inner and outer space to be of equal importance and have developed an awareness of both. The Japanese, for example, worked to ensure that both spaces were balanced, that the inner space was stabilised by the outer while the secure inner space provided a backing for the outer. The Indians of Asia, however, concentrated more upon the inner space, to such an extent that for some of them the space outside the body mattered so little that they often ignored it, and this attitude can still be seen today. Many Westerners who are oriented towards external space feel threatened in India by the poverty they see in the cities; yet, though poor to occidental eyes, those Indians, secure in their inner space, may be perfectly content.

Often there is a conflict between the two spaces. Today, there are many people with the modern 'hippy' mentality, inclined to concentrate on the inner space while taking no responsibility for the outer. Their attitude is that of expecting an income, food, medicine – everything contributing to outward security – to be provided by the state without their necessarily making any contribution themselves. The trouble is that without discipline, without development of the inner space, the outer cannot be secure. By the same token it is no good focusing only on the outer space and trying to secure it through material possessions while neglecting the inner space: we must be aware of both.

Nowadays, we have no external temple protection and instead of the usual tests we must develop ourselves in a polluted environment, and grow in the teeth of a chilling materialistic climate. Life itself is the initiation, and for many of us it is as rigorous and as excruciating as ever.

It is interesting that the Taoist word for temple is *kuan*, which originally meant 'to look': in other words, a temple is a place for observation. What the ancients were really teaching is that it is impossible for us to learn elsewhere what we are incapable of learning within our bodies. These days we have given up the security of our stone temples and have to work to build a sanctuary within ourselves. It is here, by looking within and observing ourselves, that we will work to balance ourselves.

The Church's suppression of knowledge

Unlike more explicit schools of teaching, that of the Christian Church does not reveal the mechanics of the second nervous system. Instruction is simplified and deals only with polarities: darkness and light. No levels in between are described. Indeed, hitherto, all other levels – and by other levels we mean such gifts of psychic sensitivity as clairvoyance, telepathy and healing – have been explicitly forbidden, dismissed as deceits of magic and sorcery, works of the devil, branded as heresy and witchcraft and, in earlier times, punished by death. To put it as plainly as possible, the Christian Church speaks of a way of channelling energy into the body directly through white light, that is, through harnessing the higher vibrations. Not only is this a difficult thing to do but much of the pure joy is lost if, for example, the idea of seeing energies around human beings and plants is dismissed. Rushing to the absolute is a bit like going in a fast car to your destination without enjoying the scenery on the way: in order to tune into white light successfully you have to raise your vibrations to a very fast rate. One way to achieve this is by leading a good life. Most religions exhort us to lead good lives, yet fail to explain why; instead, the nature of the drill is to catalogue all the things we must *not* do. The fact is that by living in this way we can change our vibrations, not so much through cleansing, exercising, praying and meditating as through sharing, loving and being beautiful. Yet just as a television set will not function if the power is of insufficient voltage, so it is with us. The only way to obtain power is to have a system of gathering more energy: the faster we vibrate, the more energy we produce and the easier it is to touch upon higher dimensions. But what is not explained is that in order to quicken our vibrations in the first place we will probably require an additional charge of energy. If our own system is not dynamic enough, we will need help; we will need to boost our own supply through the use of ritual or chanting or the collective energy of groups. To a certain extent, church services did (and do) provide a means of boosting energy, just as the Christian sacraments were instituted to sanction the major events of biological existence: the sharing of food (in the Eucharist); sexuality (in marriage); childbirth (in baptism); sickness (in anointing); and death (in funerals). But a vast store of knowledge has been suppressed, and before we continue we need to understand why this is so. The reasons are political, as we shall see.

The early Christians

Since the second century AD the orthodox Church has worked hard to establish an institutional religion. The original idea was that since no members of later generations would have such access to Christ as the Apostles had enjoyed, every Christian believer should look for knowledge to the established Church, to its gospels according to its Apostles, and to its bishops. Here was a hierarchy through whose authority all others must approach God; the laity should love, honour and obey the bishops as though they were God.

Now we know that if we are able to control our energies consciously we can obtain enormous powers: we can mesmerise others and make them worship us, take over human beings and enslave them. (We have only to look at the followers of certain modern gurus to see the truth of this.) The last thing the Church wanted was the chaos that was felt might come to pass if an enormous number of people started to realise their powers. Already many of the early Christians

5

had completed certain initiations and had very strong minds. Tertullian writes:

> We have now amongst us a sister whose lot it has been to be favoured with gifts of revelation, which she experiences in the Spirit by ecstatic vision amidst the sacred rites of the Lord's Day in the church; she converses with angels and sometimes even with the Lord; she both sees and hears mysterious communications; some men's hearts she discerns, and she obtains directions for healing for such as need them.[9]

Many early Christians were able to heal and speak in tongues; they had the power to alter their level of consciousness so as not to feel pain; to pass into hypnotic states and leave their bodies before being consumed by fire or wild animals – and in view of the many kinds of excruciating torture faced by Christian martyrs, including being scourged, flayed alive and fried in iron chairs, this was perhaps just as well.

For instance, Polycarp, Bishop of Smyrna, was martyred on 22 February 156. Before his death he was bound to a stake ready upon the pyre:

> A great flame flashed out and we to whom the sight was granted saw a marvel; and we moreover were preserved to the end that we might tell the rest what came to pass. The fire made the appearance of a vaulted roof, like a ship's sail filling out with the wind, and it walled about the body of the martyr in a ring. There was in the midst, not like flesh burning, but like a loaf baking, or like gold and silver being refined in a furnace. Moreover we caught a fragrance as of the breath of frankincense or some other precious spice.[10]

Eventually, since his body could not, apparently, be consumed by fire it was ordered that he should be stabbed with a dagger. Upon this a dove came out from him, and so much blood that it extinguished the fire. Another Christian martyr, Blandina, put to death in AD 177, was, it seems, filled with such powers that those who took turns at torturing her

6

became absolutely exhausted. Her mangled and gaping body was finally suspended from a stake and exposed as food for wild beasts, but none of them would touch it and it had to be taken down, later to be fried in a pan and thrown in a basket to a bull.

The Gnostics

The persecution of the early Christians by the Romans is famous. Less well known but equally vigorous was the campaign that was waged by the Church against any Christian group whose beliefs threatened to be subversive to clerical authority. So here, on the one hand, was the orthodox Church, an enclosed world of priestly intellectuals devoted to the rule of thought, struggling, with ever-increasing political power, to change mankind, while, on the other, were the Gnostics, who held that all who had reached Gnosis transcended the Church and the authority of its hierarchy. Unlike the knowledge so esteemed by orthodox believers, Gnosis is not primarily rational but an intuitive, reflective process of knowing oneself. To know oneself, so the Gnostics claimed, was to know human nature and human destiny, and to know oneself on the deepest level was to know God. Original creativity was considered the mark of anyone who became spiritually alive. He had to express his own perceptions and insights: anyone who merely parroted his teacher's words was considered immature. It is no wonder, then, that the orthodox Church viewed the Gnostics as undesirable, and volumes of vituperation were levelled against them accusing them of sorcery, magic, carnal goings-on and goodness only knows what else besides.

For nearly two thousand years Christian tradition has preserved and revered orthodox writings denouncing Gnosticism, while suppressing the Gnostic texts themselves. Many of these texts have recently come to light, having been discovered in 1945 in a cave near Nag Hammadi in the Upper Egyptian desert. Among the diverse works found are secret gospels, including those of Philip, Mary, Thomas, the Egyptians and Truth (all of which were in circulation during the second and third centuries), myths and magic, sacred chants, instructions for esoteric practices, and mystical poems with such titles as 'Round Dance of the Cross' and 'Thunder, Perfect Mind'. What these texts reveal is that the Gnostics, in their turn, denounced the Church, whose bishops they declared to be 'waterless canals'. They claimed that they themselves were the true Church, accusing the rest of being outsiders, false brethren and hypocrites. 'The Testimony of Truth' attacks ecclesiastical Christians for being dealers in bodies, senseless, ignorant and worse than pagans because they have no excuse for their error.

These Gnostic writings speak of illusion and enlightenment rather than sin and repentance. Jesus comes as a guide who opens access to spiritual understanding: when the disciple attains enlightenment he becomes his equal. Gnostics speak of the feminine element in the divine, celebrating God as both mother and father. In all, they are remarkably oriental in character. One of their teachers, Monoimus, says: 'Abandon the search for God and the creation and other matters of a similar sort. Look for him by taking yourself as a starting point. Learn who is within you who makes everything his own and says, "My God, my mind, my thought, my soul, my body." Learn the sources of sorrow, joy, love, hate . . . If you carefully investigate these matters you will find him in yourself.'[11]

Gnosticism, then, rested on personal experience and personal union with the divine, a belief that not only undermined the bishops' authority but actually made the bishops redundant. What the orthodox Church needed to establish was a theological system which was outward looking and allowed no personal interpretation on the part of individuals. And so was laid the foundations of our outward-looking Establishment, whereby the individual is encouraged to look outwards to authority rather than within himself and introverts tend to be jeered at for being narcissistic, for sitting around contemplating their navels. The Church was helped considerably about its business by the emperor Diocletian, who in AD 303 undertook to destroy all Christian documents; when the Christian emperor Constantine later commissioned new versions, this enabled those in charge to revise, edit and rewrite all the material as they saw fit. The

New Testament is essentially then a product of the fourth century, certain works being assembled for inclusion and others ignored or expurgated.

We cannot leave the Gnostics without referring to their belief in reincarnation, which has been called 'the lost chord of Christianity'. Gnosis and reincarnation were to be carried on as central beliefs by one of the main heretical groups to suffer persecution during the Middle Ages, namely the Cathars or Albigensians. Others who perpetuated the secret knowledge were the Knights Templar, troubadours, alchemists, freemasons and Rosicrucians. Officially it is held that the Church has denounced all belief in reincarnation; indeed, it is widely accepted that in AD 553, under the emperor Justinian, the Fifth Ecumenical Council cursed the doctrine of the pre-existence of souls: 'If anyone assert the fabulous pre-existence of souls, and shall assert the monstrous restoration which follows from it, let him be anathema.'[12] Although reincarnation and the pre-existence of the soul are not synonymous terms, a belief in previous lives on earth infers future ones also. Yet lately there has been some debate as to whether or not it can be shown conclusively that the Church has officially forbidden all belief in reincarnation. Head and Cranston argue[13] that since for a number of reasons neither the pope of the day nor a considerable number of bishops attended the Council and therefore did not approve the anathemas, the doctrine was not officially confounded. Whatever the verdict then, it is certain that growing numbers of clergy now speak favourably of the new interest in reincarnation.

The second nervous system

Perhaps the most important development in the idea of evolution is awareness. In the beginning, as creation crystallised into solid levels of matter and hydrogen became fused into ever-denser solutions, organic life began to evolve. Gradually the kingdoms of minerals, vegetables and animals developed, growing at each stage in terms of resonance and mobility so that at the lowest level we have the mineral kingdom dependent upon others for its mobility while at the top we have man, who enjoys freedom of movement and free will. Here is the concept of evolution as a continual procession of higher forms, with an ever-heightening sense of awareness, evolving from lower forms; always the vision of things evolving towards the light. We have to remember that everything is developing, every energy form we see: planets, stones, crystals, and plants. In every kingdom, from minerals and plants to animals and humans, different levels of sensitivity and mobility are unfolding. 'I feel in myself a life so luminous that it might enlighten the world and yet I am shut in a sort of mineral,' wrote Honoré de Balzac, encapsulating the essence of evolution. This is really what the whole of creation is: an essence which has existed in various ways through various cycles, mainfesting on physical levels in order to be reawakened and become aware.

At this juncture it is useful to cite some contemporary scientific observations. The physicist David Bohm speaks of matter as frozen light, of mass as a phenomenon of connecting light rays that go back and forth freezing themselves into a pattern. The more highly evolved a species the more complex its biological capacity to use light. As Milner and Smart explain,[14] it was the response of plants to light that gave rise to the development of organs for perception of light and so to an awareness which would bring with it an awareness of this perception. In this way 'vehicles' were formed which to begin with functioned automatically; then, little by little, as humans incarnated they took control of their own functioning.

Each individual cell has an aura and a level of awareness; even the amoeba generates light and exists with an awareness of self that causes it to react to stimuli. Fish are capable of communicating with one another on telepathic levels using acoustic waves, but they are still simple creatures and their energies are used only in the performance of basic functions. For a creature to be able to negotiate on higher levels it has to produce a system that is capable of receiving faster vibrations and set up a field of resonance which will enable it to preserve and use them; and as we move higher up the scale we can see a definite pattern of expansion, from the fundamental instincts of survival to the higher qualities of love and creativity. We can perceive a definite pattern of growth towards awareness: 'awareness of awareness' as Milner and Smart put it.[15] Primordial energies really have only one aim: for everything to reach a point at which it can sense everything and become universal – cosmic. This highest state of cosmic consciousness brings with it an awareness in which nothing in the entire universe is separate from anything else. As with the view from a mountain, the nearer the top, the wider the horizon. On reaching the summit of consciousness we experience a state for which there are no words and in which there are no limitations; words have specific meanings, and are by their very nature limiting. We can only refer to these states in the way we know best: we can call them being part of the Christ-consciousness, in unison with God.

Primitive man was extremely aware of his environment. It can still be observed that certain wild animals, and the few human beings that remain in their natural habitat, retain a vital protective system which allows them to know psychically if predators or strangers are approaching, to sense beyond the body and tell if something is creeping up on them. We have only to read Laurens Van Der Post's lovely books about the bushmen of the Kalahari[16] – or the few remaining members of that people – to see how such men use their natural senses in order to gather food and forecast the weather and the future. Ever since we began wearing clothes and enclosing ourselves within the comparative security of buildings and cities, this second nervous system has lost its external protective virtues and gradually become less sensitive. Because the external system was no longer required to act so strongly, the inner system began to develop and our mental faculties took over. Some people do retain a natural ability to react instinctively – being able to predict earthquakes and hurricanes, for example – while more and more of us are becoming skilled at using pendulums and other devices to dowse for water, minerals and other energies, but much of our original surface skin awareness has disappeared. The wearing of shoes means that the feet have lost much of their sensibility – most of us walk unconscious of the earth's vibrations – and it is really only the hands and arms that maintain a perceptivity and are used by some healers as antennae to perceive the vibrations of their patients. Part of training in the martial arts is aimed at making one aware of the subtle layers or skins of energy emanating from an opponent standing some distance away. But for most of us the natural properties of the body have been pulverised by our civilisation, stormed by our intellect and the result is that this marvellous system, which ought to operate quite spontaneously, often works only to a faulty degree.

The system, which passes along and beside the central nervous system, has been known and used for hundreds of years in the East, where a knowledge of the meridians and vital points of energy is employed in mystical and medical practice. Only recently has progress been made here in the West. Research in America conducted by Dr Robert Becker[17] at the Veterans' Administration Hospital in Syracuse, New York, has come up with the theory that there is a second nervous system, previously unrecognised by science, which parallels the one we are all familiar with. Two biological mysteries originally aroused his interest: why no creature higher up the evolutionary ladder than the salamander regenerates entire limbs and why the healing of bones is the only truly regenerative process remaining in higher animals. Over the years Becker discovered it was possible to regenerate bones and tissues in species other than the salamander. By applying electrical stimulation to the amputated stump of a frog's foreleg he succeeded in regenerating a completely new limb: new bone, new nerves, new elbow socket, new cartilage and all. He has published over 130 articles and papers explaining his theory which, on the one hand, to conservative ears sounds highly contentious and, on the other, seems like a revision of our understanding of the basic nature of life. In 1978, Becker was nominated for a Nobel prize. This second system, he maintains, controls growth, healing and the regeneration of bones, springing into action when the skin is damaged, and helps to explain how hypnosis, acupuncture and some pain-killing drugs operate. It carries direct currents and works like an analogue computer in order to control growth, healing, regeneration and the transmission of pain. At present the view is held in orthodox scientific circles that cells are specialised in the

12

performance of certain functions and do not change, yet Becker's studies suggest that these cells can be reverted to a primitive state, made to multiply and then differentiated into new cells of any type. Such a system, he reasons, would need amplifier points to boost the signals. Sure enough, not only did he locate these but he also discovered that they corresponded to the majority of traditional acupuncture points. This modern American theory ties in with the Chinese concept of acupuncture and also with the esoteric teachings of India and Tibet, which speak of energy junctions or centres known as chakras, that relay energy along the meridians. A vast amount of research has been done, particularly in Germany and the USSR, into modern techniques of acupuncture. It is not intended to discuss this at length here, but a case from the USSR will serve as illustration. One scientist, Viktor Adamenko, has invented an acupointer: a pencil three inches long which is powered by batteries. The pencil is moved over the skin, and a bulb inside it lights up when it connects with an acupuncture point. The variation in the glow indicates whether or not a person is healthy.

This second nervous system responds to, and corresponds with, the cosmos and operates through major and minor centres of energy which are known either as chakras or acupuncture points, depending on the culture. Although it spreads in an intricate web throughout the body, it is only at the surface of the skin that we can link up with it tangibly. Seven major centres govern the major glands of the endocrine system, while minor auxiliary centres control the other organs and are situated all over the body, including the palms of the hands, the soles of the feet, the knees, elbows, hips and shoulders, as well as at hundreds of tiny points all over the skin's surface. All these points are simultaneously receivers, assimilators and transmitters. They are vortices capable of holding and gathering energy, of absorbing and using different types of energy, of transmuting energies and sending them out again transformed. The chakras are transforming stations: their task is not only to act as amplifiers bringing down higher energies to physical planes but also to transform the rates of these energies so that we can absorb and use them correctly. This is how, on physical levels, we are able to exhibit higher values such as wisdom, insight, emotion and thought. In order to have emotions at all we have to modify the energy, otherwise forces from the mental planes would enter the physical simply as ordinary physical vitality.

When chakras are stabilised they allow a reservoir of energy to be gathered, but the amount we are actually capable of collecting depends on ourselves. If one centre is faulty it will colour the one above and the one below. Each chakra operates at a slightly different frequency from that of its neighbours and has slightly different ways of accumulating energy. The top centres should be quicker and subtler than the lower ones; but often this is not the case, and coarse, heavy vibrations can appear in all centres. The opposite also applies: the base chakras can be quickened. It is possible, then, to drink in energy and light using the surface of the body. The chakras are attached to the spine by stalks which have roots, the overall impression being that of a plant. Energy is sucked through the roots into the flower-like mechanism and released like a fountain. We are able to attract good and bad forces depending on the state of our chakras, and the subsequent interaction propels the chakras into a circular motion. Part of the mechanism is used for opposing things that affect us in a negative way, such as negative thoughts, bacteria and viruses, so that we can transform and release them. In the case of diseased organs, the disease is often thrown out of the larger centres into the smaller, ancillary ones and then out on to the surface of the skin so that cleansing can take place. A remarkable experience of the composer Stockhausen deserves mention here.[18] In a series of published conversations he states that he is capable of going into certain parts of his body and that he sometimes has a very precise experience of the body's individual cells. He has been able to feel the exact moment that a bacteria or virus entered into him and known moments when he was able to chase it straight out again, throw it out by trying to change the chemical structure of the cells.

Each chakra is composed of interpenetrating levels and each of these levels links again to higher levels. It is the inner core which has the ability to release and gather. In the centre of the chakra is a point at which energy passes from the higher planes to the physical, and here there is both a white hole and a black hole. This double-hole phenomenon is not unusual, for it permeates the whole universe and infuses it with new energy. Energy is sucked into the black hole and channelled through to the chakra, and the first manifestation of this emerging energy is the white hole. When the chakras are about to open, the energy increases until a strong centrifugal action forms an opening. It is important that the strongest points of the chakra should maintain a firm attraction towards one another so that when the energy decreases they are able to resume their original pattern; should a centre open too soon and the energy surge too violently, the points of attraction may not be strong enough and the chakra may not close up again, a situation which is neither healthy nor desirable. All centres of energy have stronger points in them which attract and co-ordinate the weaker points. If the stronger points diminish in any way and the centre is left to function without them, it will become unbalanced. Whatever the level, if a centre opens before points of energy are established, it will be unable to operate correctly. The opening of the centres throughout the body will lead us to accomplish things we have never dreamed of – but it is important to proceed cautiously. The opening of these energies can cause a person to react faster, but his muscles may not be able to stand the strain and may tear. The opening of energies should always be approached systematically. The body is a beautiful instrument, here to help rather than to hinder us, but it has to be properly trained.

Each chakra, as we have seen, has a certain pulse rate: some vibrate quickly, some slowly, depending on the way the person uses his body. The shoulder chakras, for example, usually move faster than those in the hips, except in the case of runners and dancers. One way of looking at the body is to see each cell as a whorl of energy, imagining that human beings are composed of whorls of active energy. If we look at various kinds of electric fire we see that the elements they contain are spiralled; this is similar to the coiled energy within the chakras. Some electrical elements are fine, some much thicker; and in the larger types of generator, the cables, or wires, are thicker still. Tiny sparks of electrical energy are contained in each whorl, and in the same way within the acupuncture points energy moves in spirals. If the spiral is either too tight or too loose, the energy will not flow properly.

Another suggestion is to look at human hair. We can see that certain individuals have thick, springy locks while others have lank, fine ones. If we examine the various textures of hair belonging to different races it will give us some idea of the various textures of energy to be found within the chakras. Different races have different energy tendencies. Some energies are fine and loose; some thick and tight. The looser the system, the more languid the person will be, the tighter the system, the bouncier. It is interesting that those people who live closest to the sun – in the tropics, for example – have hair which is extremely curly; accordingly they have a tightly coiled energy and a heightened awareness of their outer space. An African will respond immediately to being touched, or to anyone who approaches him. With races living in areas with little sunshine, the whorl of energy is looser. The British, for instance, are often described as cold and uncommunicative. They take much longer to warm up, to spark, compared to, say, Italians and Spaniards, whose feelings flare up immediately. Of course, as races intermarry the whorls become mixed and less particular.

To return again to the subject of evolution, we begin to realise that both the microcosm and the macrocosm consist of larger and smaller centres of energy, the dynamic nature of the universe is evident not only in the smaller dimensions but also when we consider such things as stars and galaxies. Through telescopes we can observe the universe in ceaseless motion, clouds of hydrogen gas contracting to form stars, expanding spirally to form planets, gigantic explosions, black and white holes; galaxies cluster in rotating spheres, spirals and discs. The cosmos possesses a kind of nervous system: something happening in a far distant planet touches the whole cosmos, just as someting happening in one part of the body touches the whole person.

At the beginning of this century, with quantum theory, physicists made the breakthrough which, in principle at

16

least, should have bridged the gap between science and religion and is concisely explained by Fritjof Capra in *The Tao of Physics*.[19] Matter has been discovered to be nothing but a form of energy. It contains no isolated lumps; everything in the universe appears as part of a complicated, interconnected cosmic web. Capra describes the beautiful experience he had on a beach when he 'saw' cascades of energy coming down from space in which particles were created and destroyed in rhythmic pulses, he 'saw' the atoms of the elements and those of his body participating in this cosmic dance.[20] In the best temple tradition, his vision was helped on its way by what he calls 'power plants'; thus what he had hitherto experienced merely through graphs, diagrams and mathematical theories he was now able to 'see'. Matter is continuous, dancing, vibratory motion whose rhythmic patterns are determined by the molecular, atomic and nuclear structures. The atom itself is no more than an area of space wherein extremely small particles move around the nucleus bound to it by electrical forces; in other words, the atoms that go to make up matter consist almost entirely of empty space. Everything is a form of energy capable of being transformed into other forms of energy: sand, rocks, water, air – everything is made up of vibrating molecules that consist of particles interacting with one another, creating and destroying other particles. The earth's atmosphere is a continual flow of energy going through a variety of patterns in a rhythmic dance of creation and destruction. All things are aggregations of atoms that dance and by their movements create sounds. It is the interplay of the force of electrical attraction between the positively charged atomic nuclei and the negatively charged electrons that gives rise to the variety of structures and phenomena in our environment. The interaction between electrons and atomic nuclei is the basis of all things.

As everything is interlinked we can begin to sense that if we explore the atom we shall learn a great deal about the cosmos. We begin to sense that without realising it we are always forming centres and groups of some kind or other that gather or release energy. Each person on earth is a potential light-transforming centre, and the most important thing about him is the quality and degree of light he is able to bring into his body. Every group gathered together creates a bigger transforming potential. Every concentration of human beings, every city, town or village, is in a sense a chakra, and, whether large or small, takes part in the ever-changing patterns of energy on earth; it possesses stronger hubs of energy such as churches and universities, and smaller ones such as houses. The earth, too, has its own energy centres which attact energy from the cosmos, and veins of force connecting them like meridians, known as ley lines. It is worth mentioning here that when we form groups we have a choice: we can use places where the earth energies are depleted, and if the group energy is strong it will replenish the earth at these points; alternatively, if our group is not so strong we can give it a boost by using places that are powerful. Our job is to infuse all matter with spirit, to inject everything we deal with with light and love; and we should look at everything we touch with a deeper level of awareness, trying to sense how many levels we can meet.

As we evolve we begin to sense an increasing awareness of self. Like a plant growing towards the light, we must eventually unfold to the stage where we respond to every kingdom and become universal. We are returning to the same electrical system that primitive man used, though he employed its external form: the purpose of evolution is to wield both the external and internal forms. Being universal means being able to prevail over every type of structure; it means being able to incorporate various types of higher energy into the body and understand them. It means arriving at the stage reached by such spiritual leaders as Christ and Buddha, to the point of being fully evolved within the atom where matter can be brought together and bodies reshaped – and here we might recall the studies of Becker. Christ manipulated the atomic structure when he raised the dead and manifested loaves and fishes; he actually changed the chemical patterns of things using the highest levels of his mind. A universal being is able to penetrate right through you, know your mind, read your heart, bring you nearer the universal flow. When you are with such an essence you feel at one with animals, plants and stones; you have a real sense of being in

18

love and feel yourself part of all matter, all human beings, all religions. When we reach universality we love everything and are everywhere; we can be in one place and manifest in another. Modern gurus often appear who claim to be Christ, the Virgin Mary, even God himself – claim, that is, to be the Truth itself rather than a consciousness which is linked to the truth. They often produce things out of the ethers, materialise in several places at once, levitate, raise the dead and peform all kinds of acts that are marvellous to behold. Yet such signs and wonders do not mean that they are a Christ or any other kind of god or goddess. Many ancient texts – among them Patanjali – stress the dangers attached to such powers, which will block real spiritual progress. No doubt if you develop along these lines you will succeed in becoming very rich, but eventually the force of gravity will pull you down and trap you, leaving you back again where you started. In the long run it is really pointless to acquire such gifts and then misuse them. Christ himself was, as we know, tempted three times – and the meaning of these temptations will be discussed later.

The bodies of man

Man manifests in a number of vehicles, and basically a human being consists of seven levels of body between which the chakras serve as gateways. Though interwoven, these vehicles may be used independently of one another, each having the ability to gather a particular kind of vibration on which it functions best. The subject of these subtle bodies is a highly complicated one, and a full discussion of them would require a book in itself. It is only possible to give a simple outline of it here.

The lowest, densest and most familiar vehicle is the physical body, the wastepaper basket at the end of the line, as it is sometimes called. When we have complete control of our physical body we are able to communicate efficiently with our higher bodies. Any abuse or misuse of the physical will limit our potential, and any weakness on our part will hinder our progress; thus it is helpful to strengthen our physical body so that it can assist us in our spiritual work. We should think of our body not as our self, but as a vehicle we are using that gradually has to be transmuted until it becomes light and starts to lose its material structure.

The etheric body is a direct replica of the physical body. It is an energy field which interpenetrates, supports and conditions the physical body; a kind of scaffolding composed of innumerable fine lines of force crossing and recrossing each other which can speed up, slow down or go into a neutral state, employing various wavelengths and interactions with the cosmos. Where many lines cross a major chakra occurs; where only a few, a minor. If you pursue the life of virtue advocated by all religions, your etheric will be pure and beautiful; equally, if you lead a messy one it will grow contaminated, congested, coarse and heavy until eventually it will destroy the physical. The task of the etheric body is to invigorate the physical one and pour into it transmuted energies from the earth and cosmos which should stream freely through its subtle conduits in the same way that blood flows through the arteries.

The astral body vibrates at a higher rate than both the physical and etheric. This is the desire body which experiences emotions – pleasure, pain, love and hate – and, with its appetites and moods, moulds the physical. It is important to distinguish between positive and negative desires. The desire to change, to evolve and help others, is positive, while the wish to over-indulge oneself with sex, food, drink and selfish happiness is negative. When a person's chakras open he can use the astral body to function beyond the physical; but if he misuses the astral the etheric will be coloured, which in turn will influence the physical. Similarly if the body is sick, the etheric is infected, the chakras close up and the astral will be blocked.

Deeper still within the core of the chakra system lies the mental body, again penetrating the other bodies and not, as might be imagined, existing merely as a small compartment in the brain. The mental body is actually an intricate arrangement consisting of four levels, but it is unnecessary to go into this in detail here. The mental body evolves through our learning and gathers to itself all those things that are worthwhile. Its task is to balance all the other bodies so that energies can be focused efficiently. Energy follows thought, and our spiritual evolution depends on how and where our thought is focused. The Gnostics taught that the lamp of the body is the mind. 'Acquire strength,' says *The Dialogue of the Saviour*, 'for the mind is strong . . . Enlighten your mind . . . Light the lamp within you.'[21]

At a certain stage in his development man needs to create, make things out of nothing, turn shapeless energy into something he can recognise to which he can relate. He needs to work with and create symbols and archetypes: limits, territories and boundaries wherein he can feel secure. When dealing with the formless there always arises a difficulty in communication. As Fritjof Capra explains so succinctly, religions, and Hinduism in particular, clothe statements in myths that are full of magic and involve the creation of a vast number of gods and goddesses whose incarnations and exploits are the subject of fantastic symbolic tales.[22] Zen Buddhism, on the other hand, makes use of paradoxical statements intended to make the student realise the limitations of logic and reason. Like all generators of power, the mental body depends for its efficiency on how well it is used. The imagination is a tool for healing and for sensing the invisible, and if we spend our energy on fantasy – sexual or any other sort – then it is wasted. For example, if we make mental visits to the kitchen to raid the larder or, alternatively, take intellectual trips batting ideas backwards and forwards, our willpower may never be able to lead us to the wisdom and beauty that is available.

Thought-forms

First and foremost we should understand the composition of a thought-form and how to deal with it. Thoughts are actually shapes, with their own colour, sound and smell, which are impressed on the etheric (and are quite different from entities, which will be dealt with later). Every invention – every plane, every train, every city – started out as a thought-form, an invisible shape in the ether, before manifesting physically. Milner and Smart[23] describe how, by employing a certain process, they are able to photograph hitherto invisible etheric forces. They discovered an organisation of structures in the interweaving forces of energy that registered on their photographic plates and resembled many of the primordial shapes to be found in nature. Their examples resembled wireworms, centipedes, ferns, flowers, jellyfish, caterpillars, thorn bushes and the branches of certain plants. They also discovered a similarity between plant structures and the organic structures of animals, such as the nerve and blood systems and tissue structures. Their conclusion is that the original formation of matter came about when interweaving etheric circuits congealed into interweaving veins of minerals. Etheric forces, in other words, are basic and universal and underlie all formations of material worlds. All physical shapes have an etheric double which is invisible to the ordinary eye.

In the case of thoughts, the impression made in the ethers depends for its intensity and durability on the strength of the mind that formed it. A strong mind can project a thought-form which may hang about cluttering up the atmosphere for hundreds of years. The control of thoughts was one of the most important lessons of the temples. All thoughts had to be made potent and all unnecessary ones dissolved so that neophytes did not have to waste their attention on psychic housework, on mopping up the ethers. And it is as important these days as it has ever been to police the kind of thoughts we have: if we entertain bad thoughts we pour garbage into the air, which can cause as much nuisance on etheric levels as piles of rotting rubbish do when left lying round crowded cities. This is why cleansing and purification play such a central role in all religions. Just as the physical body should be well kept, without surplus pounds of flesh, so the other bodies should be kept clean, free of superfluous ideas and thoughts.

The ancients knew how to use thought-forms in many different ways. They knew how to boost their energies by the use of groups, animals, trees and stones. Energies released from stones are particularly strong. Stones gather energy from the sun and radiate it at certain times of day: stone circles, for example, deliver their energies just before sunrise. The ancients would assemble at dawn and gather the huge forces that were then released. In Egypt, massive statues of the gods were carved and at the moment of radiation the priests would fashion a huge replica of the god. The bigger the statue, the more potent the force and the stronger the thought-form. This was an extremely powerful thing to do because the god would be with you, you would feel its presence wherever you went until eventually you became subservient to a huge thought-form which followed you about and appeared in your dreams. This was one of the reasons why the gods were so powerful and why in the Bible we are commanded not to worship graven images. Idols were actually recharging instruments: an individual could link up with their energy and so boost his own.

In the same way that the sun charges stones with energy, so does prayer. If people pray and chant in front of statues, this can make the statues potent. An example of this is to be found in the images of Radha and Krishna which form the focal point of the ritual of the Hare Krishna cult. Disciples dance, chant and bang drums before these huge dolls, fan them with peacock feathers and offer them food several times a day. The result is that these images transmit a tremendous energy, but, like all idols, they can become invasive. If you open up your psyche to anyone or anything that is constantly being recharged through worship, you may end in psychic slavery – and here lies the danger of constantly focusing your attention on photographs or images of gurus which you will therefore be continually recharging.[24]

Another modern example of the influence of thought-forms can be seen in sport. Sensitive sportsmen, footballers perhaps, may sometimes be infected by negativity emanating from the crowd and become inhibited in their playing. This can explain why some of them are able to play twice as well at home, where everyone is for them, than when they are away and the general feeling is against them. Thought-forms can certainly influence us, and it takes a strong person – or one who knows what he is doing – to overcome this difficulty.

There is a well-known theory that the Russians may be developing techniques of psychic attack. Henry Gris and William Dick,[25] who went all over the Soviet Union gathering material, discovered that that country has a multimillion

23

rouble research programme into parapsychology incorporating a number of secret psychic research laboratories. Gris and Dick tell us that experiments cover a variety of subjects, ranging from UFOs and abominable snowmen to healing, reincarnation, hypnosis and regression. They state that many of these are concerned with character alteration and with the correction of such problems as stuttering, bed-wetting, asthma, frigidity, alcoholism and high blood pressure, as well as with persuading individuals that they are famous singers, pianists, intellectuals and chess-players. Evidence received from CIA agents stationed behind the Iron Curtain leads us to believe that the Russians are now able to influence the behaviour of individuals at long distance: to alter people's emotions, make them fall asleep in meetings and even kill them by the use of psychic powers, visiting their victims with sensations of anxiety, suffocation and dizzying blows on the head. The theory is that nowadays it is less the nuclear weapons that are the focus of interest than the control of those in charge of such weapons; though it is also believed that Russia, like the United States, is investigating the possibility of tracking submarines by the use of clairvoyance and detonating or exploding missiles in mid-air by the use of psychokinesis. In any case, the ability to deal with thought-forms is as important as it has ever been; even if we are not having to contend with political invasion, our own crowded cities are hotbeds for hundreds of miserable thought-forms which infest the atmosphere and trespass on our own personal space.

The aura

Using the tools of science, it can be shown, experimentally, that in certain conditions physical bodies can be altered and that the medium surrounding the body is in fact an electrical field. This aura, this protective electromagnetic field surrounding the body, can be used as a weapon for the transmutation of thought-forms. It is composed of radiations from all the bodies of man and can be seen as a great cosmic fountain through which energies from the earth and cosmos link up with us. The Russian, Semyon Kirlian, is famous for his system of photographing auras, which currently is being developed for use in the diagnosis of diseases such as cancer and mental illness. Kirlian, who was originally a repairman and mended anything from bicycle lamps to X-ray machines, worked with his wife for years in a tiny flat.[26] All his equipment was kept in his bedroom, which by day served as a laboratory; by night, the black reconstructed Tesla high-frequency generator acted as a coat hanger. In the course of his research Kirlian often received shocks so powerful that he would fall, stunned, to the floor. His wife died in 1971, one of the victims of science: exposure to high-frequency 200,000-volt electricity eventually destroyed her, the cause of death being deterioration of the body, which had encountered too much stress affecting the nervous system. In any event, Kirlian's equipment revealed auras, seas of shimmering light, bright patterns of activity, existing over the surface of leaves and other objects. By photographing a human finger it was discovered, too, that the human aura is dependent for its quality on the psychological and physical condition of the person concerned.

There are no limits to the boundaries of any of us, and each person's aura is different. That of a vibrant individual may extend beyond his house, while that of someone who is less radiant will fill a correspondingly small part of it or merely the corner of a room. Generally speaking, the etheric double stands a few inches from the skin and the astral extends from one to two feet, while the mental body extends from a few feet to an indefinite distance depending on the psychic abilities of the individual in question. The bigger and stronger, the more beautiful the auric space, the better, and the more dedicated to people, the more the aura grows.

Whatever its size, an aura is never still: it probes the atmosphere constantly like a blind man feeling with his fingers, and, depending on what it is penetrating, alters from moment to moment. Exchanges occurring on human levels can be quite extraordinary. Some people are naturally capable of transmuting attacks with the sensitive outer edges of their aura. When one individual projects a thought towards another, the energy unwinds from that thought and projects

25

itself. The ancients thought of projections as snake-like, attacking their victims; so imagine a snake coiling itself up and unwinding, then striking its prey. This represents the energy patterns which coil around a person in the mind and the aura. Providing the energy field is strong and high above the head, every time a thought-form meets it that thought-form will be deflected or dissolved. If a thought-form does penetrate the auric space, the energy from the surface system will often dissolve it. But those individuals who do not possess strong systems will need to contract their auras for protection; subconsciously they will be afraid of anything negative. This causes a grey wall to form around them, and frequently negative thoughts will hit this and either hang about on the periphery or become absorbed into the earth. Those with strong chakras, on the other hand, have a diamond-like reflecting mechanism and everything directed towards them bounces off again although not necessarily transmuted; the thoughts strike a mirror-like shield and return to sender. If someone throws a negative thought-form at you and you are conscious of its being there, you can transform it and send back love; in this way you will melt down some of the dark or unfortunate thought-forms in that person. Should a snake-like vibration come towards you, you can either open up the energy fields above the head or make the energy in the feet feel stronger; you will then be able to take what is coming and reshape it. You might see it as a water lily, floating, or allow it to dissolve, letting it form a beautifully clear crystal in the mind. You have to remember that what you receive in a thought-form is energy and that any energy can be changed and transformed. It is important that we do not allow an accumulation of negative thought-forms in our auras; too many of these can be dangerous for they become reflected in the chakras and pollute them. We need to go to the country, spend time by the sea; holidays are a help, providing they do not involve travel from one city centre to another. All through history rituals incorporating sacrifice, dance, chanting and music have been the means of drumming up energy to be used in many ways, one of which has been the dissolving of thought-forms. Strong vibrations in various parts of the earth also help to disperse thought-forms, as do open spaces, thunderstorms, mountains, human beings with strong energy fields and various breathing exercises.

Exercise

Try to set aside a time when you can empty your mind and concentrate on your aura. We have to meditate and imagine that we ourselves and the space around us are clean and pure, that our space will touch everything, making that clean and pure also. So first of all, sit down and try to feel the space around you. How does it feel? Does it feel clear? Or does it feel cluttered? Does it feel uniform and strong? It is important that the aura should be balanced: do you feel either too high or too low in the auric egg? Sometimes the aura can bulge overhead, which means there is not enough energy in the feet; the space beneath the feet is essential for taking in energy and cleansing negativity. Perhaps you have absolutely no idea how your space feels? In this case you have a blockage due to a lack of energy going in the right direction. It is not until you raise your consciousness and use your energies constructively that you will notice what is going on around you. Start with a simple strengthening exercise of breathing round the aura – it is good to practise this first thing in the morning. First, stretch well; unless you begin by stretching and allowing the body to align, abdominal breathing can make your abdomen protrude. Next, get the initial breath right. Exhale strongly; then inhale steadily, filling the lower part of the lungs. This is accomplished by bringing into play the lower part of the diaphragm, which, as it descends, exerts a gentle pressure on the abdominal organs and pushes forward the front walls of the abdomen. Try to keep the lower part of the abdomen from expanding too far, and fill the middle part of the lungs, extending the upper chest and lifting it. In this final movement the lower part of the abdomen will be drawn slightly in, which supports the lungs and helps to fill their upper parts. Note that this breath does not consist of three distinct movements; the inhalation must be continuous, the movement uniform. Try to exhale slowly: make this movement as long as you can, holding the chest in a firm position and drawing the abdomen in a little, lifting it up slowly as air leaves the lungs. This is the basic breath for all breathing exercises.

Now, breathing in this way, breathe seven times up the back of the body and seven times down the front. Feel what you are doing, and go out a little further each time. Try to feel how far you can go on each breath, forming the primordial egg shape. Then in the same way go up the right side of the body and down the left, still making the egg shape: up on the in-breath, down on the out, seven times.

When you have done this, try to think of the space around you as clear, as having a beautiful sound and scent, taste and quality. If you are continually emptying the space around you and thinking of all the beautiful things you can possibly imagine, a great deal of negativity will flow away. The tree of life, water, mountains, plants, ladders, spirals – all these can be symbols used for raising the consciousness. Imagine you are cleansing the aura by thinking of the area around you and under your feet. Be aware of the chakras in your feet, which need to relax very deeply: these react on the forehead, the top of head and the neck. Relax between the toes, and cup each heel with the mind. Stroke the feet with the fingers of your mind, and feel the different types of energy there growing comfortable and beautiful. Think of warm water, soft grass, morning dew – until the feet let go. When the heels relax, the whole of the feet relax; you can feel energies rising up through the ankles.

Go into the knees, releasing all negativity from them until they are soft and relaxed, their small centres opening like stars. Go into the hips, and sense the chakras radiating in a strong, relaxed way. Relax the energies and concentrate on the pull of energy from the hips. Move into the abdomen: relax the organs, releasing all tensions and pressures. Go into the lungs and try to feel the exchange taking place within them; feel them white and clean, their radiations recharging the whole body. Everything starts to feel alive and well. The energy streams in, flows into the toes, into the spine like a deep river; and the spine reacts by opening and relaxing and allowing a radiant energy to flow up from the earth running up to meet the descending heavenly energy. At the top of the head, imagine a golden fountain drawing down energy from the cosmos so that you become a huge centre of light. Now you have transformed yourself – your space, your part of the earth. Try to think of vibrations coming out of the body like beautiful wavy hairs. Imagine you are stroking the aura: it is almost a feeling of combing dishevelled hair, and you feel all around you that the space is newly combed.

The cleaner you are, the more energies will change. Energies from the cosmos are drawn towards you; energies around the earth will be attracted to you. They will come from all directions and be transmuted by you, and those you do not need will be absorbed by the earth.

CHAPTER TWO

The Basement: The Excretory and Reproductive Areas

Animals often express emotion through their tails. Dogs wag theirs with joy, while cats bristle and stiffen theirs like bottle brushes in fear or anger. The tail, in other words, is a vehicle through which excess energy can be discharged. Moreover, when an animal swings his tail backwards and forwards he is collecting extra energy. If a dog wags his tail on seeing you, this produces energy at the top of his head to which he may react by jumping up with delight. When a cat wags his tail, however, he is getting ready to attack: a different reaction, but nevertheless still a pumping of energy into the head. So the tail is a kind of energy pump. Human beings no longer have this faculty either for pumping energy or releasing tension. What happened was that when man's tail disappeared his energy became condensed into a coil at his coccyx; in other words, the tail is the Kundalini unwound. In the case of a human being, the energy can get stuck here and set up an itch, a state of high tension, until eventually it may explode into some form of violence. If, on the other hand, something excites that energy, causing it to unwind and rise up, this will recharge all the chakras in turn, until it reaches the head.

Climaxes

We are all familiar with the lovely heady feeling of being 'on top of the world'. Most of us long to feel this way, to feel different, yet do not know how to achieve it. What many of us fail to realise is that everything in the body is geared to raising the energies higher and higher. Even the Church gives instructions for raising vibrations, in the prayer: 'Lift up your hearts to God', in other words, 'Raise up your energy, your love, to white light'. Most of us, though, are trapped deeply inside our bodies, pulled down by the force of gravity into the human frame. It takes heroic courage to break the bounds of security. In order to liberate ourselves we have to be prepared to expand beyond the limits of our personalities.

The raising of energies may be effected in a number of ways. A sensitive person can sometimes manage this just by holding the hand of someone compatible. As a rule, however, the only time human beings are able to enjoy the kind of realisation that goes beyond the body is through sexual orgasm. During sex the base centre is quickened by pumping energy. This energy starts to move, rousing all the centres in turn towards the head. A sexual climax is a huge release of energy up the spine to the head, and for a brief moment we are able to stop feeling self and to appreciate beyond. In meditation, the same energy is lifted up, often mounting much higher. There is in Rome a statue which portrays St Teresa sitting in ecstasy: the mouth is open, the eyes are rolled upwards. This is a different kind of climax: a mystical one which does not require another person for boosting the energies.

When the base chakra is very strong it animates the other chakras and a powerful energy goes through the roof of the mouth, hitting the pineal and pituitary glands. Once this happens, the force opens up the top of the head and there are no limits. One of the reasons yogis swallowed their tongues was that they wanted to be sure of being able to return to their bodies.

Where ordinary sexual intercourse is concerned, the pumping of energy in the base chakras is a necessary ingredient. Those who have active centres often reach a climax tremendously quickly, while those of a more sluggish nature sometimes have difficulty in reaching one at all. If a man vibrates very fast and has a premature ejaculation this can mean that he is ready to move on to a higher form of love. It might be a good idea if he experimented: using the energy for learning how to control his centres in order to stop them releasing so fast. He could try raising the energies in subtle

31

ways which do not involve physical contact. Some couples do not even need to lie in the same bed, they have such closeness on different levels, such a high degree of telepathy. We need to realise that making love is just one way of exchanging energy. Animals throw out vibrations to one another all the time. In the case of human beings, if one looks across a room at another and suddenly feels weak at the knees it means that a kind of love spark has connected them both. That person has woken up, it could be said. Normally, of course, energies are not exchanged as strongly as that. If we sit beside someone and feel madly dizzy, we are not necessarily falling in love; the fact is that we are sitting near a powerful energy field which is causing our brain levels to change. Lilla once knew a yoga teacher whose energies interacted with her own to such a degree that they actually produced sparks. So if you touch someone and sparks fly, this does not mean you should rush into bed together; instead, you might try feeling that energy going up your spine and allow it to express itself naturally without going through all the physical rigmarole.

Of course, caressing another's body can be marvellous, and healing as well. Apart from anything else, stroking the skin alerts many of the acupuncture points. Being massaged brings with it something of an understanding of the movement of energies within the body – but being stroked on deeper levels by higher vibrations is something else again. Here the vibrations pass right through you and touch you on other levels so that it seems as though you are being touched all over. It is possible to feel like this when someone touches you physically, yet it is seldom that the whole body melts away into higher planes. It is this inability to be part of another that makes us need sex again and again. The hunger for a relationship really means that somewhere within us there is a longing to lose ourselves and raise our energies up beyond the head. Often the reason we crave sex is that we are unable to get it. When someone is with us all the time we are continually exchanging energies with that person, and the sex urge diminishes. Some people worry if either they or their partners do not feel like making love, yet what they may not realise is that something beautiful could be happening: it is possible that they have grown together and are exchanging

32

on other levels, thereby making a basic sexual exchange redundant.

Sometimes another person's body can be a tool, one of the only ways we have of expressing ourselves. The style of person we like making love to will depend on our own style. The type of man who enjoys sport and physical activity will usually want a woman with an alluring figure, while a similar type of woman will appreciate a strong, well-built partner. The higher up we go, the less physical appearance matters so far as sex is concerned. If a man or woman has had a lot of unhappiness or illness, then he or she will seek a partner with healing vibrations so that sex will bring with it a sensation of being comforted and healed. Whatever we ourselves lack we will look to another to supply.

The use and misuse of sexual energy

Sexual energy is just one of the manifestations of the vital forces of nature: 'the green fuse' as Dylan Thomas called it. The ancients viewed sexual energy as something to be worshipped and linked that worship to nature. Sexual energy was offered to the gods in order to appease them, and it was through sacrifice, which released blood and a huge energy from the victim, that the gods were placated. There is an interesting difference between making love out of doors – in a forest, on a beach, in a field, when the sexual energies are dissolved and returned to nature – and indoors. Making love indoors, no matter how primitive the buildings, means that the energy is contained and that patterns are created that encourage repetition. In ancient times, as energies began to be used constructively, temple initiations became more complicated and the basic energies began to be used by initiates for spiritual growth. It was found helpful for the community to join male and female energies – helpful, too, to go through binding ceremonies so that land and possessions could be divided and children provided for.

The point of having another person is for boosting and sharing the release. The yearning for a relationship really means that somewhere within us lies the need to raise up energies. An experience that is purely sexual bombards the

33

base and makes the chakras move too fast either to control or to be aware of what is happening; it releases too much energy, which is therefore impossible to harness for use at the top of the head. Indulging in sexual energy purely for pleasure will prevent us from opening up our consciousness, although for some people it is still the only way they have of expressing themselves at that moment. As we grow in awareness we learn that sexual energy – like all energy – can be transmuted.

One of the main points of Tantra was that the man should control his ejaculation so that the energy of his sperm could help him in esoteric practices. The woman, too, was trained to draw up her energies and maintain them so that her partner could gather energy. Her discipline was to hold herself in a highly aroused state, thus producing energies which her partner could drink in and so be able to rise up to a state of ecstasy. Eventually it was found that this boost of energy from another person could open up past lives, together with the ability to see into the future, and many high priests exercised these techniques in the performance of their duties. One of the secrets of Tantra was knowing which parts of the body to excite and exactly how much. In this way one person played upon another like an instrument, creating different notes and sensations. Here is an ordinary solo example of the way the parts of the body affect one another: if you take your little finger, place your opposite hand around it and press, this should excite your excretory and reproductive areas. The next finger should affect your abdomen and solar plexus; the middle finger the heart; the index finger the throat, eyes and forehead; while the thumb should bring an overall sense of peace, which is one of the reasons for thumbsucking in young children. Bringing the finger tips of both hands together will raise the vibrations and create a high note in the body. So through the arts of Tantra two people aimed to work together using various ritualistic movements to raise the sound of their bodies and accordingly their vibrations. One way to raise the vibrations while making love is to imagine your partner as a god or a goddess. This bestows an archetypal energy which he or she would not otherwise possess: by making love to the archetypal male or female you will actually be raising your vibrations.

Sex therefore has many aspects, and as with everything we should neither be obsessed with it, nor should we be addicted to the idea of sensuous fun. If our attitudes are wrong and we use our energy in an unhealthy way or over-indulge the sexual area, illness will ensue. If, on the other hand, we suppress sex altogether, we may invite an overwhelming desire for it, just as if we go on a diet we may long to overeat. If we fail to use the sexual areas altogether, repressing all sexual urges, this can lead to fantasy, which is as much a waste of energy as promiscuity.

The first thing we should ask ourselves if we are strongly oriented towards sex is why we need it so much. If we are not able to practise a sport, to transmute, control or release the energy, then we can become overcharged. If we have no energy going up the spine, that is if we have a lot of heavy base energy stuck in the lower chakras, we will feel perpetually on heat and this itch may become so intense that it can explode uncontrollably into violence. Such a person will have no idea what he is doing, and in extreme cases may even commit murder. In the same way, if an individual is very negative he may be attracted to those with very pure energies, such as a young child; this can open up all his energies, which may erupt into uncontrollable lust and anger leading to violence. Too much energy with no control – no accompanying instinct for healing or preservation – creates a maniac.

Although masturbation is a way of releasing tension it can, in excess, be debilitating, and there is a danger that the bodies of those who practise it a great deal will be unable to react well to external stimuli. With masturbation there is only stimulation of the base chakras and no energy exchange. The Victorians, of course, exaggerated its dangers, yet it is true that masturbation at a young age can cause problems since it expends vital energies that are required by the system for growth and development.

Our modern society, with its advertisements based on sex and its carnal preoccupations, encourages national sexual obsession. Regular orgasms are considered the consumer's right: everyone should want and have more of them, along with more of everything else. The result is general neurosis

35

and promiscuity. Promiscuity can affect energies in subtle ways which are not generally recognised. To be able to deal successfully with energies that change continually depends on an individual's stability, also on his adaptability. When we sleep with someone we absorb that person's vibration, and for a brief space of time the two of us mingle together. If a woman chooses one who resonates to her vibrations, her energy will not be excessively strained; but if she is forever turning from one man's vibration to another's, the constant changes in her energy fields will set up stress and may eventually be one of the contributing factors of cervical cancer.

Another thing: the more promiscuous we are, the more cords we set up. A cord always, eventually, has to be worked out and broken. We do not realise that cords can be set up not only by making love physically but by making love mentally. Many men, when attracted to someone, lie in bed and think about that person sexually, creating a strong thought-form. It is possible for some people to make love in their minds and give an orgasm not only to themselves but to the object of their attention as well. A girl may suddenly feel herself becoming sexually aroused for no apparent reason. If, say, a model appears in the press either naked or scantily clothed and a man masturbates while looking at the photograph, he is capable of forming a cord on the etheric levels, of projecting a thought-form; with the result that the model may feel sexually stimulated, even raped. The more neurotic a person, the more he is likely to project unpleasant, aggressive thought-forms.

Darkness and light

Light is the oldest, most pervasive metaphor used to describe spiritual experience, while the age-old battle between light and darkness – or good and evil – is an evergreen source of material for the writer. The popularity of horror films, videos and detective stories in which the good and the bad seem to be fighting is really symbolic of the forces of gravity versus the forces of light battling within us and trying to balance out. Opposites are the two sides of the same reality,

36

extreme parts of a single whole, different aspects of the same phenomena; 'Let the light penetrate the darkness, until the darkness shines and there is no longer any division between the two,' runs a Hassidic passage. By the act of focusing our attention on any one concept we create its opposite, and thus we spend our lives divided.

We have, as we know, in our system a black and a white hole in every chakra. We can see this in the famous Yin and Yang symbol which represents the core of the chakra system. Two currents of vital force, male and female, are represented by black and white flowing one into the other in the shape of two petals, each curving round the other like two embryos in a womb. So, in every chakra we have a gathering and a releasing mechanism: on the one hand, a dark male Yang centripetal force gathering, contracting, assimilating, organising and earthing, and on the other, a light female Yin centrifugal force expanding, dispensing and lightening. Without this gathering and releasing of energy there would be no life or movement. Both the force of gravity and the force of light are expressed as forces in nature; both these forces are neutral energies which may be used in any way we choose, and both are indispensable. The heavier vibrations are essential for earthing: without them we would become dizzy and be unable to undertake any practical, physical work. Gravity and the heavier particles are therefore valuable assets, but, like everything else, not to be caught up in, and we should think carefully how we can use all the things around us that are linked to gravity – even heavy marble can give the impression of lightness if a sculptor infuses it with energy. Light is not incompatible with the darkness of matter, as the Egyptologist Isha Schwaller de Lubicz says, 'for matter would not exist if the light were not already formed within it'.[27] Just because something is intense and gathers energy does not mean it is negative – indeed, gathering energy is something we do naturally all the time – but where it goes wrong is when there is no proper exchange for any reason and nothing is reflected or given back. Negativity gathers when people hold on, unable either to give or to reflect, therefore becoming unbalanced – or too Yang. The darkness is only destructive when there is something wrong.

Its function then is to cause you to disintegrate until the energies are able to gather together and you are capable of coming out of the darkness you have created for yourself and going towards the light. People may not realise that if they enter a negative phase in their lives the chakras will automatically start to gather energy in order to break it up. The breakdown occurs as soon as the energies reach a point at which they have to disintegrate so as to piece themselves together and return in the opposite direction. Whichever course you pursue, you must know that you have to integrate the two or else you will be thrown from one side to the other. As you go towards the light you become lighter and lighter, until on the highest plane of all you melt into light and lose all shape. With the opposite, you become denser and heavier and the energy tends to cling to the lower part of the body: extreme cases of this can be seen in mental patients who become obsessed with the lower parts of their bodies and caught up in repetitive patterns concerning masturbation and defecation. Either extreme leads to disintegration and causes the person to burn out his circuit. You cannot go towards one without recognising the other; for example, if you go towards the light, working hard to quicken your vibrations by cleansing and purifying, yet at the same time reject people who need help, this will not be acceptable to the psyche. 'If you desire the light, be sure that you will never find it except by begetting it in your own darkness,' as Isha Schwaller de Lubicz says.[28] Monks, traditionally, would enter into a contemplative examination every night so that they could review their faults objectively; they would write down those things that they felt to be wrong. It is better to let your negativity come through so that you can observe it, deal with it and release it.

It is interesting to note here that Frank Barr, a Californian physician, has come up with a theory that suggests the brain is organised by an almost impenetrable light-absorbing substance, melanin, which effectively acts as a black hole with apparent superconductor properties. Also of interest is the fact that he traces its inception to a series of ten dreams he had in 1975, while still a medical resident. These dreams were intense and archetypal, and included one of a black

Christ on a rotating cross grappling with Lucifer. The most bizarre feature of these dreams was his experience of 'a blackness that was specifically experienced as being inside my brain, during the dream'.[29]

The force of gravity

The Church has never denied the darkness; indeed, it has talked so much about light that to recognise its opposite has been essential. Some icons portray the devil to remind people of what they would look like if their energies disintegrated. These paintings are symbolic representations of the way psychics saw the heavier gravitational fields. We know through reflexology that the bottom part of the heel links with the base of the body: when the etheric stops gathering energy, the top half of the foot stops releasing energy altogether and only the dark energy is left, which appears to a psychic in the form of a dark hoof. Nowadays, because of the Kirlians' work, it is possible to photograph cancerous cells and to discern the shaggy vibrations these emit. As a person gets heavier the energy at the base of his body is released in uneven patterns that resemble the matted hair of animals. In the same way, the devil's hairy chest is symbolic of the disintegrating heart energies. His horns have nothing to do with the horns of beasts, but refer to the energies above the head which are represented variously in different cultures as haloes, lotuses, feathers, and so on. When the energies here disintegrate they all but disappear, apart from two small points of cunning at either side of the head which continue to radiate, hence the horns of the devil.

Black magic

It has always been said that powers can be had from the devil, and there are many classical tales dealing with this subject, among them the Faust legend. Yet the devil always destroys his disciple in the end. This is really the act of being destroyed by the forces of gravity. One of Christ's temptations in the wilderness involved Satan taking him up on to a high mountain and showing him all the kingdoms of the earth: these would be his if he agreed to worship the devil. Another temptation was that in which the devil set him upon a high pinnacle and urged him to cast himself down. Christ refused, indicating to Satan, who represented the force of gravity, that gravity was not a toy to be played about with: one does not levitate or perform party tricks just to show others what can be done.

Black magic makes use of the heavier gravitational fields: those forces in nature which link up with the black-gathering elements. Its practitioners concentrate on the base chakras, employing pumping mechanisms and various rituals to approach the black hole. In the beginning, everything seems fine: as you move into the black hole you open up a residue of energy, and the rituals and ceremonies, which often include stimulating sexual celebrations, may make you feel stronger and better than before so that you may be able to heal. Gradually, however, you will experience a loss of energy and find it necessary to borrow from the forces of nature, using sacrifices, stones and so on. If at any time we need help, we can get it from nature: from animals, jewels and plants. (Trees are very healing and can restore and strengthen, though the deciduous kind should not be approached when they are coming to the end of a cycle, when their leaves are falling.) But anything that is borrowed must be given back in some way. Having 'green fingers' means that the person is able to use his second nervous system to tune into the king-dom of plants and give them energy so that the plants he tends register this and flourish. People who have lower ener-gies thrive on taking energies without returning them: they become psychic parasites, living off energies without giving anything back, without replenishing nature in any way. Yet it is impossible to do this without causing repercussions. If a person takes in energy and sends nothing out, he himself becomes a black hole because by using only the black-gathering mechanism he is unable to use the white to release in a constructive way and the structure begins to break down. At a certain point of disintegration he begins to lose not only his vitality but also any degree of contact with his higher self.

The modern archetype is Dracula, who lives by gathering vital energy from women, by sucking their blood, usually from the neck. He wears a black cloak symbolising the aura, which has turned completely black. He has become a black hole and, like all black holes, he attracts and fascinates.

Hitler, who took a great interest in the occult, used this black reservoir of power. At a certain stage in his development he had to make the choice between good and evil, a choice that confronts many people during their lives. He had to choose between helping human beings to help themselves and helping them to have what he thought they ought to have. To put it bluntly, he decided on trying to alter things to suit himself. He saw himself as the universal consciousness and believed the higher masters were telling him what to do. Peter Sutcliffe, the 'Yorkshire Ripper', also thought he was being guided by the higher powers, by God himself. The point here is that in the collective consciousness there are plenty of masters to whom you can give any name you like, but primarily they are forces of energy. You can stir up the collective consciousness and gather energy by being a good and beautiful person, or alternatively gain power over others and use them as energy forces. You can persuade yourself that you are right, that you are working for the great masters. You can get a kind of obsession in which you create a master etherically; or again you may attract to yourself the heavy forces of the universe so that these succeed in possessing you and cause frightful mental disturbance.

The function of the black force is really to act as an earth to balance out the white and break things down in order to build them up again. If we keep using sexual energy and pumping it up without taking into consideration the lighter vibrations of beauty and love, our chakra system will become overloaded with heavy vibrations, the base chakra will turn black and burn, and we will experience overcharging. Just as any electrical gadget has a fuse and an earth, so we too have an inner fuse and earthing system, and if for any reason we pass too much electric current through our bodies we burn ourselves out. A symptom of this is to experience excruciating heat and to take on a heavy, prematurely aged appearance. The etheric as it pollutes itself must eventually release into the physical body, whose organs then have to take this pollution and clear it. Gradually as the etheric and physical

41

organs grow heavy, the mind and all the channels will become affected and the chakra circuit will burn itself out. In the case of someone whose circuit becomes completely burnt out, the mind becomes unable to focus and the body disintegrates.

Hell means that the person in question is too heavy to reach the higher dimensions. Having ruined his circuit by overcharging it, he experiences sensations of extreme heat – the same kind of dreams and nightmares as encountered in a raging fever. Hell is an experience shared by all who have burnt out their circuits, who experience hallucinations of roasting in barren landscapes of rock and red-hot larva. This is because when a human being misuses his energy he regresses in time and becomes caught in a span that existed before oxygen and vegetation, a period when the earth's energies were primordial. A burnt-out etheric needs hundreds of years' equivalent of our time to mend, for the vehicle has to be completely built up again.

Cleansing

As a person becomes heavy there is a tendency for him to desire to be cleansed; just as someone who becomes physically dirty feels the need to wash, so the etheric grows malodorous and the person will want to purify. Earth energies are important, and many places on the earth's surface emit beneficial radiations: the crossing of ley lines, for example. Just to walk along a ley line will bring you in contact with many strong energies which will have an effect on your auric space. Ramana Maharishi, the Indian sage, always recommended the ancient practice of walking round a holy mountain, Arunachala in southern India; as you walk the nine miles you come under the influence of various magnetic fields, which changes you subtly. A person may be attracted to the sea, to open spaces, to parks and the countryside, or alternatively to very pure human beings. Extreme cases of this are sexual perverts and maniacs who are drawn to the cleansing energies of young children. In the same way some older people feel attracted to younger energies: older men to younger women and so on. It is possible for an older person to plunder the energies of a young child or baby, and

42

because of this it is inadvisable for an infant to be handled a great deal by debilitated elderly people.

The ancient yogis understood the importance of regular cleansing, and resorted to many singular practices which seem ridiculous to Western eyes. Even within the security of temples, purging was conducted as a matter of routine. The point of church services was to clean you up, quicken your vibrations and combine your energies with those of the rest of the congregation. The Catholic mass, with its prayers, chanting, incense, candles, holy water and altar stone (which in medieval times contained holy relics), was a device for boosting the energies in order to alter the consciousness. During the Middle Ages fasting and pilgrimages were felt to be beneficial. The idea was that as you walked, as part of a group, along ley lines, repenting your sins, sharing your goods, becoming part of a group consciousness, praying and asking for forgiveness, many of the coarser vibrations were dispersed. The places of pilgrimage themselves were especially powerful, being situated at the crossings of ley lines and charged still further by the relics of some saint or martyr. Such relics were highly prized, and those of Polycarp (see Chapter One) collected at the time of his martyrdom, were considered to be more valuable than precious stones, finer than gold. One of the reasons for this is the powerful vibrations saints' relics emit. Anyone who has visited the Mevlani in Konya, where the Sufi mystic Mevlana Celel Ed-dun Rumi, founder of the order of whirling dervishes, lies with his father, son and sixty-five of his most illustrious descendants and disciples, and experienced the charge of energy to be felt there will know the reality of this. In medieval Britain the shrines of saints and martyrs were often encrusted with gold, silver and jewels. The famous tombs of Thomas à Becket at Canterbury and of Edward the Confessor at Westminster glittered with gold, rubies and other precious stones; indeed, they represented such a treasure trove that in the sixteenth century Henry VIII's officers plundered them in the name of the Reformation and carried away the spoils. The point here is that gold, silver and gemstones are, like quartz crystals, powerful transformers of energy and can be used not only in watches and radios but

43

also as instruments of healing and cleansing. The ancients, who believed jewels to be petrified energies, had elaborate ways of grouping them according to colour, light effects, thermal qualities, wavelengths, radiation, even taste and used selected gems in various forms, crushing some, powdering others and extracting their potency in water and other liquids.

The body cleanses itself etherically through exhalation and excretion. Inadequate out-breath and constipation leads to many problems. A prime cause that accelerates deterioration is when the organs of the body fail to clear. Unless stagnating energies are removed from the base of the body, healthy, positive energies are unable to enter. Food can stay inside for as long as two weeks. The bowels, mouth and nostrils – all these have to be kept clean.

Many serious diseases, including cancer, are rooted in an inability to release negativity which can arise very early in life through 'potty training'. In young children, the excretory area functions in a natural way, causing them to empty negative energies along with the bowels and the bladder without conscious effort. It is possible for someone to develop constipation by being told to do things at a certain time: this makes one hold things in. When the bowels and bladder are restrained, so is the function of eliminating negativity from the system. When 'potty-training' becomes too rigid it can upset the child and a pattern of constipation may set in for the rest of his life. Disharmony in the base centre repercusses and sends discord throughout the system.

Furthermore, our modern lavatories are unhelpful when it comes to releasing negative energies. Primitive man crouched – as many orientals still do – but in Europe this natural crouching position, which automatically relaxes the muscles, has become a rarity (and for some almost an impossibility). It is significant that, in certain modern holistic therapies for cancer, enemas have been found to be beneficial.

The ability to relax often plays an important role in clearing toxins from the body. But it must be reiterated, you have to be aware that if you are meditating and getting the body very relaxed, going towards white light, you may attract black; all your negativity may well up to the surface. It would be helpful to take the example of the ancient monks, and learn to observe and deal with it. If the negative, dark energy starts to attack you, it should be recognised as a challenge and accepted as such. Coping with our failures, seeing ourselves for what we are, is very important on the spiritual path. Many people think there is nothing wrong with *them*, that it is everybody else who is at fault. We must take a look at ourselves and examine the negative aspects of our natures. Purifying the system, even in tense situations, *is* possible. In order to go deeper into the higher aspects of ourselves we have to deal with our weaknesses. If we relax, meditate and concentrate we can release all the things that are no longer necessary and allow any under or overcharging to regulate itself, because the chakras are capable of regulating themselves providing we allow them to do so.

Just as Christ was tempted in the wilderness, so are we likely to be tempted. As we become clean, different types of energy and individuals will become attracted to us; once we raise our consciousness we will be able to help all types of negativity. But it is not just a case of purifying the body constantly until the vibrations are strong in the hope that we will eliminate temptation or be able to repulse anything negative; as we know, those with negative chakra systems are attracted to positive, clean individuals and, in extreme cases, may attack, rape, even murder, them.

Cleansing exercises

Cleansing is not just a case of sitting in a corner doing exercises; everything has to be taken into account. First of all, it is good to take a practical look at the place where you live. See that there are no negative ley lines or underground streams running beneath the house. If there is something wrong with the earth energies around you, you are fighting a losing battle; so if you yourself are unable to dowse it is sensible to consult a dowser who may be able to neutralise the negativity. Are there places in your garden which are not vibrating harmoniously? Look at the trees around. Do they have any strange-looking growths on them? Are there any which are not regular or healthy? What about stagnant waters, marshland, or streams – especially if these are close to electrical circuits in the house? If you have strong energies in your feet you will be more or less protected, but if through tension the energies decrease then you will collect negativity through your feet.

If all these conditions are unfavourable, you should perhaps think seriously about moving. If this is impractical, begin by dowsing over the entire area. Next, try to see whether there are any entities or thought-forms that should not be present. Look at the objects in your home: are your possessions radiating well? Keep the place where you live as physically clean as possible so that your own energies, when pure, will make everything they touch radiate better. If you yourself are feeling negative, a good spring-clean can be helpful. Take a look at your meditation procedures. Many people meditate in one corner of the house, which makes that particular corner radiant, but then get up and revert to their usual habit of worrying all over the other rooms with the result that the rest of the house is not etherically clean. For most of us it would be better if we worried in one corner and were calm and beautiful everywhere else.

If all the people living in a house are not in tune with one another, this can make some rooms etherically dingy. Rooms are coloured by their inhabitants' auras and out-breaths, and in this way the etheric body will either be strengthened or weakened. Perhaps there is someone living with you who is not very strong etherically, so that as you cleanse they pollute: you may go round feeling exhausted all the time. Perhaps you are one of those people who can dissolve the thought-forms of others: if so, you will find it exhausting if your companions keep on forming more. Purifying the ethers of a house is important, whether you do it through love or meditation. Pictures on the walls, candles, incense, beautiful music such as Gregorian chant, the colours you choose for decoration – all these can help clear the place. Everything around us vibrates – just having a Bible in the house sends out good vibrations – so try to spread beautiful objects that radiate well through the place: jewels, stones, plants. It is worth inviting a group of people to your place to pray, meditate and work together. This makes your home a centre of light and keeps it etherically clear so that those present will gain from the vibrations; so will your animals and plants. Some animals collect negativity and are constantly ill, and the same applies to plants. If they breathe in the wrong vibrations because of you, you are slowly killing them. If the plants around you always die, there is something wrong with you: they are dying because they are absorbing your negativity.

Cleansing your environment and your body helps to purify your mind: that which is on the outside reflects within. When it comes to cleansing the chakras, the biggest block is the mind itself. Reading good books, taking the body swimming and for walks in the park or the country, going to art galleries, trying to do everything as well as possible – all these things help. By negativity and wrong thoughts we produce within the mind itself so many divisions, almost as if inside us there were different people all contradicting one another. Emptying the mind is a holy thing, but it must be refilled with right thoughts. Like a computer – it should be correctly programmed. It is essential to realise if and when you get into the grip of a vexatious thought. First, you must recognise it; then, upon its approach, which provokes such unpleasant reactions filling the whole system, you must resolutely turn your mind away and replace it with something else. This can be anything, providing it is real to you and beautiful: a rose, for example, a water lily – something fragrant and vibrant.

First sit down quietly and make quite sure that you will not be interrupted. Always earth yourself well before meditation. It is good to feel that you have symbolically bathed yourself in water, washed your hands, put on clean clothes; Muslims and Hindus are among those who go through a physical ritual of washing themselves before prayer. Make sure you are relaxed. If you are unable to relax, clench your feet and hands and let go, clench your buttocks and let go, shrug your shoulders and let go (a comprehensive relaxation exercise is given later). Start to form within yourself a positive place, a space inside where you can be. If it does not seem quiet, build it up until it is. You can make a chapel, a temple, a laboratory, a room, anywhere you can go to work, to rest, to be at home; you can put anything you like in here to make yourself comfortable, but remember that what you put in will affect you: by repeatedly imagining this room you are programming your subconscious. You may like to have around you pictures of nature and skies, beautiful, soft colours (not too much red, which is inclined to overstimulate the base centre), comfortable furniture. Now sit comfortably and do the following breathing exercise: breathing properly is essential – to bring peace to each chakra. Imagine the chakra as a beautiful gold cup which you are going to fill with love, the waters of life. If it helps to imagine love and the waters of life as a fine golden wine, then do so; imagine anything that is helpful to you. So, breathing in the correct way, breathe seven times to relax the base chakra, visualising this gold cup gradually filling. Do not make the cup a specific size; just keep it within the hip area. Start on the outside of the chakra and try to feel that each breath brings you into the more spiritual, interior aspect of that chakra. On the seventh breath you will relax the middle, which is usually that part of the chakra most in need of cleansing. Tell yourself to get stronger and cleaner, and through relaxing that part you will feel the chakra getting purer and cleaner. When you have finished you must close down the chakra. Imagine it gradually turning into a large, shining ruby, filling the area within your hips. At the end of each meditation it should gradually become natural for you to close down by giving certain signals to the psyche: by pressing the hands together, perhaps, or by rubbing them, or by stretching part of the body. Always return from each meditation through the body feeling the hands and the feet, and having a good stretch. Returning to the physical should be slow and guided by our finer instincts – to earth well is vital.

Physical exercises for the base chakra

If you feel your base chakra needs stimulating for any reason, it is helpful to rub the feet well. Make sure the legs are active and in good condition. You can use the colour red – wear red knickers, for example – and, more energetically, you can use primitive kinds of music with a strong beat and dance and stamp your feet.

Sensing exercise for the base chakra

(You can put all these exercises on tape and practise them either alone or with a group.) In the base chakra are memories of evolution and the sea. Try now to sense the sea and its terrific energy. Try to feel the difference between tuning into a peaceful lake, which is all calm and still, and tuning into the sea when it is stormy and rough. Then tune into a great waterfall, like Niagara. Feel the power there, the speed. Feel the difference between the lake, the sea and the waterfall. Now, as you breathe in, feel your breath like a wave of the sea so that as you breathe in you feel the wave swelling up, staying for just a fraction on the surface, curving and plunging down. Try to feel your stomach curving in so that you feel the abdomen move in and the wave flowing out of your body as you breathe out. Do this several times, feeling the actual movement of the waters. Feel as if you are just above the waters and you are walking or floating. Just feel the presence of the vibrations, feel them in your body; in your feet, feel the sense of cleansing. See if you can tune into a whale and a dolphin: can you feel the energy, the resonance in the water, as they contact each other by telepathy? See whether by just sitting there relaxing you can experience the different landscapes under the sea. Feel the changes in the levels of the water and see whether you can go back in time to when it was younger. If you can just feel a little, you will find changes; you may get a different feeling to the sea itself. Try to see where you are drawn, to which ocean. Now imagine you are getting into a boat. Think whether you want a fast or a slow boat, and just allow yourself to drift a little to the central part of the consciousness which is an island – somewhere a little like Iona, perhaps. Here you are going to sit down. Here there are the remains of something very beautiful. You feel a little isolated, yet at the same time surrounded by the benevolent influence of the water. Feel that here is a small monastery. Enter the courtyard and try to feel that you are now in the very depths of your inner centres. Go into the

49

cloisters, which echo with the sound of your footsteps, and try to imagine the huge old wooden door with its heavy key. Open it and go through, and look at what you see beyond. Stay there and be still for a little while. Gradually when you are ready, feel the body resuming its shape; perhaps not quite the same shape as before yet feeling quite natural. Give yourself a rub and a stretch and make sure you are closed up.

Relaxation exercise

Find a comfortable position and close your eyes. Try to feel that the room is very comfortable and very safe. Try to feel that it is filled with peace and security and that any noises you hear will not disturb you. Feel your clothes touching your body. Sense the surface of your body: be aware of the skin, the muscles, the bones. Now, in order to relax, begin with something very simple. Go up the body practising the principle of opposites: a little bit of tension, a little bit of letting go; a feeling of being tight and of being loose; of being hard and being soft. Start with the feet. Take a deep, slow breath. Breathe right in and clench up the toes very tightly; clench them really well. Then, very slowly on a long gentle out-breath, let go. Open out the toes; relax them. Go deeply into the toes with your mind; massage between them. Go deeper and deeper. Caress your instep with your mind, feel it letting go, deeper and deeper. Stroke your heel gently with your mind. Relax all tensions, all pressures. Feel a change of atmosphere around your feet. Penetrate deeper and deeper: there is a lovely sense of relaxation. Allow the contours to melt. Gradually dissolve the feet. See the feet as radiations moving and changing, so that there are no longer any feet to speak about.

Now your consciousness goes higher. Take a deep breath and clench your calves tightly. Feel your calves well; feel their outline and their form. Very slowly, breathe out and start to let go: go deeper and deeper until your legs feel longer and longer. Plunge your mind into your calves; penetrate their structure. Go beyond the muscles and bones. Gradually your legs melt into another sense of reality. Take another deep breath and feel the firm outline of your knees;

accept them. Breathe out very slowly and start to disperse everything that is negative in this area. Stroke your knees with your mind; soften them, penetrate deeper and deeper. Allow the contours to melt. Gradually dissolve the knees. When you have done that, concentrate on the buttocks. Here, once again, breathe in and clench them very well. Clench the buttocks, and when you are ready breathe out and let go very slowly so that you feel the buttocks have no tension. Relax the base centre at the very bottom of the spine. The base of the spine feels better. Feel the sense of well-being in this area. The sense of well-being is so strong that you feel borne up by a beautiful fragrance and essence. Now go into the abdomen. Summon up a good, strong breath. Breathe in. Hold your breath. Hold the whole of the abdomen very tightly. Once again, breathe out and loosen, feel all that area spongy, soft, melting.

Now take your consciousness into your solar plexus. Take a deep breath and imagine the structure, the outline. When you are ready breathe out, soften the contours, let go and dissolve your organs, muscles and cells. Imagine now a ray of sunshine shining down and turning all this area into gold: it makes you calm and radiant. Imagine all the nerve endings in the lower part of your body, all the acupuncture points there, radiating light. Everything is beautiful. The golden feeling becomes deeper and deeper. Imagine that gold energy streaming up from the base of the spine into your solar plexus: it flows on up into your heart. Your heart is melting. Feel your heart opening like a rose; look deeply into it and see the gold centre of energy. Now take a deep breath, and, as you breathe out, relax your shoulders – drop them. Go down your arms. Pour a sense of relaxation into your palms until they feel heavy. Feel the beauty of your hands: they are soft and gentle. Your fingers feel open: gradually your fingers dissolve, your wrists melt away. Your hands are transparent now – radiant whorls of energy. You feel nothing but calmness, relaxation. Now go into the elbows. Caress your elbows with your mind; stroke them. Go deeper and deeper. Go into the shoulders again, into the back of the back. Now the gold stream of energy is flowing up your spine. Feel the left and right sides of your body, balanced, correct.

51

Now relax the throat. Anything that is negative in this area is dispersing. Sense the stillness in this area now: the whole area is still and light. Your face is growing softer and softer. Relax the lips; relax the jaw. Go into the mouth and feel the energy rising up into the roof, up into the pituitary and pineal glands. Go deeply into your eyes. Try to feel that your eyes are open although they are shut. Imagine your eyes are clear – beautiful, like two pools. Imagine your eyes are like wells: you can look right down into them. Look into the wells of your eyes, deeper and deeper, until you feel you are floating. Go into your forehead, into your third eye. Feel this area. Relax the ears and the back of the head.

Relax completely. Imagine all the acupuncture points of your body opening. Your body is illuminated with pinpoints of light. It shines with hundreds of stars. Everywhere around you the atmosphere is different. Begin to feel your body very deeply and completely. Your whole body is wrapped in a beautiful glow of light. Lights appear on either side of you, at the top of your head. And now a radiant figure approaches, shimmering like mother-of-pearl. On your head it places a wreath of flowers, roses, lilies, jasmine – any flowers you like. Smell them, feel them. And as it places the wreath over your head its hands release energy. Down into the top of your head a fountain of golden energy pours like nectar; pours down, cleansing, flowing down, bathing away all negativity, all tiredness and tension, all anxiety and illness. And all these negative things are pouring out of you, through your pores. You can see them, black like mud, flowing away until there is nothing left but the clear, fragrant fountain pouring down over and through you so that you are new and clean.

CHAPTER THREE
The Abdomen

If we again consider evolution we can see how the lower chakras are geared to survival. On physical levels, the base and abdomen centres, which are closely connected, deal with the reproduction of the species together with the assimilation and evacuation of food. In primitive man they responded to patterns in nature, only coming to life at certain seasons. Festivals played an important role in the life of ancient communities: they were group efforts during which rituals were performed, designed to ensure fertility and success for everyone. Often the chanting and dancing ended in sexual celebration and a great deal of energy would be released, thereby giving nature a boost, so to speak. Ancient country dances were not just jolly ways of passing the time but a means of reviving the whole community: whirling in chakra-like circles round a maypole, for example, helped vibrations to rise. A large number of these festivals are still with us and exist in many countries; but they are only pale shadows of their former selves, for the inspiration and excitement is no longer there and the communication with earth, trees and plants has been lost.

Primitive peoples danced a lot. Dances were sacred ways of drumming up sexual energies by rhythmically beating the ground with the feet – just like modern discos, except that here the energies are drummed up for no purpose other than pleasure. Witch-doctors still dance to whip up their powers, dervishes swing themselves round forming whirlpools of very high energies, which, when assumed to music, as in ritualistic dance, can be very strong and help the whole etheric. The legendary dance of the seven veils was a closely guarded secret in the temples. Dancers started moving to the rhythm of the base chakras and gradually rose up through the centres. The veils were of colours that corresponded to the vibratory rates of each chakra, and the music changed accordingly. By the end the performers would have stripped away the negativities that had blocked the reception of higher energies.

Relaxation

Each centre has its own way of bringing relaxation to the body and mind. The base centres release through bowel movements and sexual ejaculation. With the abdomen, there are two ways. The first is physical exercise: you do a lot of sport, take a lot of exercise, sweat your guts out and get to the point where you are pleasantly tired and able to relax. What you have done is use some of the energy that your brain would otherwise be using for thought, so your mind becomes more peaceful. The other way is through eating: when you are full of food you experience a comfortable, sleepy feeling. Once again, the brain is deprived of energy that it would otherwise be using for thought, since quite a lot of effort goes into the digestion of food. Some people whose energies are overcharged have minds like dervishes that whirl in circles and so feel the need to eat continually. They crave satisfaction, and if cramming in an enormous meal is the only way they can become relaxed, then their bodies will drive them to eat a lot. The body does its best under difficult circumstances to make you peaceful, and if this is one way of getting you to relax, then this is what will happen. Whether or not you put on weight will depend on you as an individual: those with fast metabolisms can eat as much as they like and never get fat, while others seem to eat hardly anything and are plump.

Assimilation

Behind all problems lies the body's inability to cope with and release tension. The abdomen is vital for assimilating food and releasing toxins. If functioning properly, it will store energy and act as a reservoir. But, as with all centres, problems will develop if negativity is retained there. If tension is allowed to accumulate, then the digestion and assimilation processes will be affected and nervous disturbances may be felt, before meeting people perhaps, or if work, or anything else, is proving difficult. Smoking, drinking alcohol and worry – all these can affect the assimilation process. Certain medicines, particularly antibiotics, actually stop some vitamins in food from becoming released, so if you take antibiotics you should also take vitamin supplements.

These days many people have difficulty in assimilating food. What is not generally realised is that the abdomen attracts and absorbs energies, not only from the food itself but also from the environment. Modern economic methods of food production (which depend on the use of hormones, herbicides and insecticides), the energy of the earth, the person cooking the food and those with whom we share it – all these can impinge. The abdomen is closely linked to the throat and these two zones of food ingestion react with each other, so assimilation is affected not only by wrong and excessive amounts of food and drink but also by conversation and tension at mealtimes. Efficiency in assimilation will be coloured by what you see, read or think. So it is unwise to watch the television or read the newspapers while eating.

Never cook if you are in a bad temper: it shows up at once in the vibration of the food. Never discuss problems at mealtimes. It is just as important to be aware of how you eat and with whom you are eating as it is to be aware of what you are eating. Indeed, it is often not so much a question of what you eat but of what is being used by the body and how much it can assimilate. If you eat a meal that is accompanied by lively, stimulating conversation, then the energy that should go into assimilation will be diluted. Business lunches can be appalling for the constitution, causing indigestion and probably ulcers. We talk far too much during meals, mainly to cover up our embarrassment because of the inadequacy of our communication. In monasteries, silence is traditionally maintained and eating is usually performed to an accompaniment of readings from the Bible or some other elevating work. The idea behind the practice of accompanying meals with music is that a great deal of lovely energy will resound around the room and relax the body.

Blessing the food

All ancient cultures blessed their food, and the ancients had special stones for making food potent. Before a meal these stones would be touched or the food itself placed on particular stones in order for it to absorb their energy. With the aid of Kirlian photography it is possible to see that when bread or water is blessed it radiates better. We can see that during a meal changes take place and energies manifest in the body which were not apparent before. So blessing the food can certainly change the energy patterns; but we must realise that if we are in a bad mood and we bless things we may only be releasing our negativity into them. Really the greatest blessing we can give our food is a relaxed body with which to receive it, so as to absorb it properly. The idea of saying grace, or a prayer before meals, was to put the body into a peaceful state. There is another thing: saying a prayer can cause a change of brainwave which may give us the opportunity to link in with the elemental kingdoms (see Chapter Seven). Contacting elementals produces more energy not only in the food but in ourselves. So if you eat in a restaurant and you sense that the vitality has gone out of the vegetables – that, say, the peas on your plate are debilitated – it is possible to tune into the fare and regenerate it.

Fasting

Negativity may lead us to smoke, drink and eat too much especially rich and heavy food. If the body does not cleanse properly it needs either a purification diet or a fast. Fasting is important for ridding the body of accumulated waste in the abdomen: the clogging of waste materials causes gathering of heavy energies. During initiations, fasting was a means of seeing whether the initiate could control, not just the assimilation of his food but also his mind. Initiates practised silence while fasting so that both the abdomen and throat were controlled. Moreover, through fasting, the lower centres, which are normally very heavy and earthed, become light: the earthing system is weakened and the metabolism speeded up.

Vegetarian diet

In the past, vegetarian diets were used for purification before initiation or, if a patient suffered a serious illness, he would be put on a meatless regime for cleansing, but at the same time he would be programmed; this means that uplifting ideas would be introduced into his consciousness. This is significant: vegetarian diets produce faster energies, and as more energy moves up the spine it is possible for the individual to become in touch with subconscious levels. It is not just feeding the body that matters, but also feeding the consciousness. If we follow a vegetarian diet but pay no attention to our thoughts, we may allow ourselves to be possessed by negativity. Generally, carnivores have less energy going up the spine; their energy is altogether heavier, especially if they consume meat in large quantities, so negativity does not penetrate so deeply. If we are vegetarians we should therefore look very carefully at the negativity in us. Many people's systems are still geared to eating meat and may require adjustment in order for a vegetarian diet to become compatible. If someone inclined to be negative gives up meat, he may find that his physical energy becomes low and that because of this faster brainwave he gets dizzy turns and hallucinations. In other words, to switch abruptly to a vegetarian diet is not always advisable; it is sometimes better to continue eating meat in small quantities and to reduce it gradually week by week so that the system is able to adapt.

Allergies

The underlying cause of all allergies is the misuse or abuse of the body, which is unable to cope with toxins. Yet unless we know something of a person's background, unless we can find the point at which in this or a previous life his symptoms began, we will not really be able to discover what created his inability to assimilate certain vibrations. Patterns can recur if circumstances repeat themselves: if in a past life a person was allergic to someone or something it is quite possible for that allergy to return if the circumstances are similar. The faster a person's metabolism, the more strongly he will react to his environment and be affected by the seasons. With the coming of spring, for instance, if the lower chakras have been quickened everything may begin to irritate the nose and throat, which are, as we know, closely linked to the abdomen. The person's breathing may be affected, and it can be impossible for him to clear the sinus. When the stomach is strong and contracted the nasal passages tend to be far more open, but when something is wrong with the anatomy or the bone structure is slightly out of alignment, then the out-breath will be very bad. If you sit beside someone with sinus trouble you will see that they hardly seem to be breathing at all. They are not relaxing, so that the breath is not doing the right thing. A typical asthmatic is one who, through inhaling in short bursts and not exhaling properly, has an enlarged ribcage. When circumstances arise in which he has to breathe out, he finds he is unable to do so properly: perhaps he reacts to fur or pollen which causes him difficulty in breathing. He enters a room, sees a feather perhaps, or a cat, picks up the influence – and his lungs seize up. In such cases, the chakras, instead of going fast or slow, arrive at a state in which they stand still. One part wants to speed up, the other to slow down, and the result is critical: the person is precipitated into a state of shock, unable to breathe. What he needs to do is exercise his body and teach himself the mechanics of breathing and relaxation. He needs to concentrate on exhalation. Breath that comes in short bursts rather than deeply and slowly may also lead to the establishment of minor infections. These are not always strong reactions, just continuous small ones. The irritation can lead to the formation of pockets of germs, which means that the person is constantly fighting infection; so long as a part of his sinuses remains unhealed the least thing will trigger it off. In the beginning, perhaps in early childhood, some shock may have occurred which created conflict; and this eventually caused an infection to take hold somewhere very deep.

Allergies can sometimes be caused by too much variety in one's diet. Dishes are rarely cooked plainly these days; as a rule they contain eight or more ingredients. Meat, for instance, may have tomatoes, peppers, garlic, onion, mushrooms, spices and wine added to it; and if we enjoy elaborate

1   During initiation, the candidate entered a tomb and was put into a deep trance so that he could experience his death in order to be reborn. This vignette from The Book of the Dead of Neferrenpet shows the soul, or consciousness, represented by the bird with the human head, flying down to the tomb on the right. On the left the initiate rises up and walks away, fully conscious and spiritually awakened.

2   Massive statues of the Egyptian gods gathered energy from the sun which could then be used for different purposes.

3 Prayer can charge up statues in the same way as the sun. Images of Radha and Krishna are the focal point of the modern Hare Krishna cult.

4 Bernini's statue of St Theresa in ecstasy.

5 This temple sculpture from Khajurāho is a physical expression of the male and female, positive and negative energies wound round each other.

6 In Lilla's chart the same energies can be seen spiralling internally through the body. The idea of representing this sexually was to show that the circuits have to be excited before the energy can rise up and be released at the top of the head.

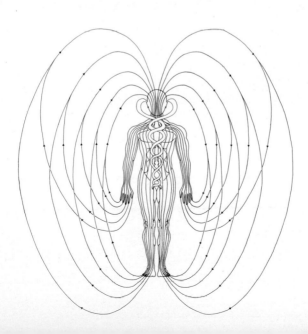

8 Detail from a Chinese dish showing a group of sages with the Yin Yang symbol, representing darkness and light.

7 The shell shows the universal energy spiralling upwards to the light.

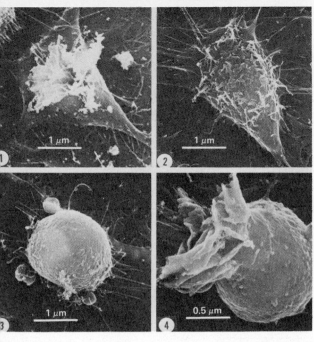

9 With modern systems of photography it is possible to chart a healthy cell's disintegration into a malignant state.

10 The devils' shaggy bodies, portrayed here in a fresco from Pisa, are a symbolic representation of the same process: the disintegration of energies as a result of a person becoming heavy through being unable to release negativity.

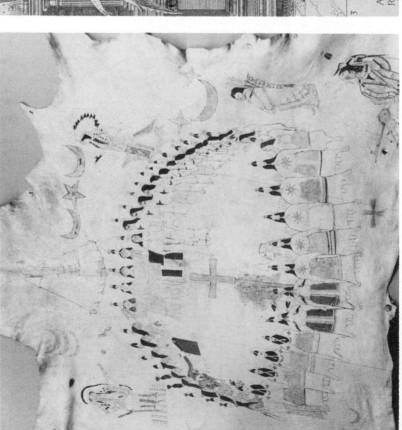

11 A Red Indian Sun Dance. Dances were sacred ways of drumming up energies; moving or whirling in chakra-like circles helps vibrations to rise.

12   The acquisition of gold has always made people powerful, but most who amass material riches end by being pulled down by the forces of gravity, symbolically

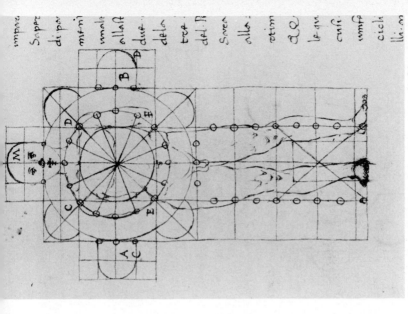

14 A plan of a church by Francesco di Giorgio, drawn in harmony with the proportions of the human body.

13 Typical fears are of spiders, birds, mice: tiny things.

15 The highest vibrations move in waves and appear to psychics as shimmering feathers, represented here in this fresco from Cefalù Cathedral in Sicily as the wings of angels.

16 Vignette from The Book of the Dead showing the weighing of a heart against a feather.

food and entertaining we may dish it up with separate vegetables in rich sauces, preceded by soup or soufflé followed by cheese and/or coloured puddings. Like sex, eating has become a pastime. The point is that each ingredient is linked to a different elemental and if we make too many connections these can affect the digestion. Lilla knows someone who was cured of colitis simply by reducing the variety of food that was consumed.

Ulcers and cancer

When the slowing down of vibrations occurs as opposed to the quickening, ulcers – which are the plague of businessmen – and cancer can appear. This kind of illness tends to make the energies even slower. The process of assimilation becomes sluggish: the stomach and other digestive organs are not well co-ordinated, the gastric juices and enzymes fail to function properly. Acidity sets in and the system breaks down.

Anorexia

Anorexia may be caused initially by a desire to be thin, or alternatively may stem from a particular worry or problem. Whatever the cause, the centre above the abdomen, the solar plexus, becomes highly overcharged and gathers more and more energy so that tension is produced in certain parts of the body which makes it almost impossible for the person to swallow food. Often the victim bursts into fits of crying when confronted by meals, and tensions mount, to be reflected in family and surroundings; later the patient suffers from a seizing up of muscles in certain areas and an inability to release them.

Practical ways for strengthening the abdomen

It is good to treat each meal as a sacred ritual so that we can take in higher energies to which all the centres will respond. Changing into clean clothes and putting candles, beautiful covers and flowers on the table may help to create the right atmosphere which will turn a meal into a ceremony for

59

gathering energy. We should try to fill every space with the feeling of peace and make each meal an act of communion. We should try also to tune into one another and into the room where we are eating, to give our bodies a chance to communicate with us. The only time intuition really comes into play is when women are pregnant and experience cravings for extraordinary things to eat. Until quite recently we ate according to the seasons, and some diets still involve a strict adherence to seasonal food. Yet what is right for one person is not necessarily right for another. We need to be more attentive to nature. We have cycles in a day, a month and a year, times when we are weak and when we are strong. There are times when we react more to what we eat and times when we react less. We have to listen and do what is right for us. We should avoid rushing through our meals. We should not be set into eating habits. Primitive man ate raw vegetables and tough meat, yet nowadays we hardly use our jaw muscles: gnawing bones is out, and most of our food is excessively tender. We should eat things raw, and we should experiment with different ingredients, trying those we have not tried before. Remember that the same food will taste different each time, depending on the hour of day, the mood and the conversation. If we are cooking for a family, we should try to sense what they need: so many eating and assimilation problems stem from childhood and parental attitudes at mealtimes.

Try to approach food with dress sense. What colours are you wanting? Where does your attraction lie? Warm colours are important: carrots, oranges, red apples. Be aware of advertisements and of why they attract you. Colours have a very definite vibration, and what may make one person healthy may not work for another. Be aware of the packaging and do not buy things simply because you are drawn to their wrappings.

We have reached a stage where people are using the abdomen very badly. We need to keep the body stretched, which helps this area to sink into its allotted place. Many who sit badly do not have their abdomens in the correct position at all. If the abdomen and its muscles are strong, this will help you to be a positive person; there is a theory that if you are strong in abdomen and belly you cannot be destroyed.

Lilla's experience in this connection is interesting. Many years ago she drove her car out of a side road and nearly had a head-on collision. This gave her a bad fright which affected her for quite some time. After a few years of doing karate and yoga, the same thing happened, but by then she had very strong muscles and all she felt was a spontaneous contraction and release – no feeling of nerves at all. It is significant, too, that Tofik Dadashev is one of the few Russians interviewed by Gris and Dick[30] whose health does not seem to have been wrecked by his excursions into the paranormal. According to these authors, Dadashev specialises in complicated feats of thought transference and is able to read and control others' minds. The point here is that he trains for this work with the intensity of an athlete training for the Olympics, rigorously exercising his jaw and abdominal muscles and practising breathing exercises. Breathing properly, as we know, is essential to the correct functioning of all chakras, and it is particularly important for the abdomen to ensure proper absorption and assimilation.

Breathing and stretching exercise for the abdomen

Place your hands – or your mind – on the upper abdomen and take three breaths, feeling that you are opening out. The first thing to watch is that on the in-breath you feel that you are using the upper portion of the abdomen rather than the lower. If your nostrils are blocked, you can take the right hand, place it under the left armpit and press; and then do the same thing with the opposite hand. This is also excellent for asthmatic attacks. The next thing to realise is that if you take an in-breath that is quite long and an out-breath that is shorter you will never have a flat stomach: the out-breath has to be longer than the in-breath. If you have a tendency to take in breath very quickly and not to release it strongly, the impetus of your breath will extend your ribcage and abdomen, so the best thing to do is to forget the in-breath and just think about the out-breath. And when you breathe out always be conscious of feeling you are strengthening all your muscles so that they make a nice little corset. Take a deep breath, putting your hands on your abdomen, and be aware of your out-breath and of tightening your muscles. The second time, concentrate only on your out-breath. Now have a really good stretch and place the hands above the top of your head and do exactly the same thing noticing the difference: your waistline has gone down, while your body has gone up. Bring your hands down very slowly, keeping your body as high as you can. Put your hands back on your abdomen, take a deep breath, and, when you are ready, breathe out further: your stomach should go in further still. Very few people are the right length: we all tend to sag. Stretching is vital because each time you stretch an energy tends to go up. Put your hands on your ribcage now, and look to see how wide you can expand it while breathing in and out three times. Make sure you are moving, and remember that when you breathe out you have to contract. Try to make a tidal wave which opens up everything you have touched. On the out-breath bring in the abdomen first so that you feel it is playing a part in flushing out the breath. Always remember that the out-breath is more important than the in-breath.

Physical aids for strengthening the abdomen

Nature is very helpful for strengthening and stimulating the abdomen, so the following are good: gardening, digging, walking, the martial arts, bodily exercise in general.

Exercise for strengthening the muscles

Sit in a strong, upright chair with supports, your bottom right against the chair back, and hold on tightly, either to the seat of the chair, top of the legs or bottom of the chair back (depending on the type of chair). Keeping your legs straight, raise them as high as you can and then move them up and down in a scissor movement. Move your bottom into the centre of the chair and do the same thing; then move right to the front of the chair and repeat the movement again.

Exercise for heightening awareness using the sense of smell

Begin by sensing the smells which make you feel more aware of the base area. Starting with the reproductive area, try to feel the perfumes there which are slightly heavy and rich. From there move up and try to sense the smell of food cooking – onions, bacon, garlic, bread baking – and all the warmth and security this engenders. Go higher, and now you can reach the essence of sunshine and nature. You can get energy just from sitting indoors and smelling flowers and trees. Flowers react well to being smelt, so you can try performing this exercise physically. Take a fragrant flower, or several different kinds of fragrant flower. Smell them, and then see if you can recreate their perfume. Then in your imagination hold them in your hand and stroke their petals; just bend over them and gently sense the scent. Try again, and see whether any particular perfume, any particular flower, appears: we all have affinities with nature that are very deep, and a particular flower can often be your special way into the elemental kindom. Now sense the fresh air and the sea. Try to feel the blue colour: blue makes the aura feel big and brings a sense of lighter, headier scents. Try to open up to the essence of water and air; try to feel that kind of smell, the freshness, the salty tang of sea water. Now, in your mind go into a church or place of meditation and see if you can create the fragrance of incense – sandalwood, perhaps – the smell of candles burning, of fire. It is quite possible to feel a smell in a way that is almost tangible. Now imagine various textures of cloth – hessian, linen, velvet, silk – and bring with them their various scents. Sense that your aura is becoming beautifully translucent and that you feel the whole of it clean and shining. There is a marvellous sense of stillness, yet also a feeling of being extremely alive. Try to feel the taste in your mouth; sense the feeling of taste, relax the tongue, the back of the throat. Try now to sense where your auric space is in the room, where it ends. Remember that just as the aura has a particular sound, so it has a smell. If something in your life goes wrong, if you are scared or unhappy, that smell will change.

CHAPTER FOUR
The Solar Plexus

Primitive man's solar plexus would erupt only when required for fight or flight; then it would close down. Originally this area was used specifically for dealing with the environment, for accumulating the energy that man needed for pursuing his food and running away from danger. As civilisation advanced and human beings, feeling safer in groups, gradually settled into farms and communities, the fight or flight mechanism was no longer so necessary and the energy began to manifest in other ways. As less energy was required for moving about it began to be used for the left side of the brain, and, as written language came in, man lost his ability to memorise well. Nowadays our problem is that we are unaware of anything happening in the solar plexus until we suddenly experience all kinds of strange churnings. If, for example, you are shy and stand before a large audience feeling you have nothing to say, you will acquire enough energy to run for miles; but it is also possible for the solar plexus to gather enormous energy before you go on stage, where it is capable of releasing such brilliance that you will dazzle the audience with your performance.

While the base chakras are geared towards group awareness and being part of everything, the solar plexus is the area of individuality, the centre of the 'I' consciousness: the feeling that everything in the world revolves round 'me'. This does not mean that the 'I' consciousness is unimportant; on the contrary, this 'I' consciousness, this ego, is vital. As we grow more sensitive and quicken our vibrations it is possible for us to become 'spaced out', and it is essential to have a strong sense of individuality to return to. The more capacity you have for spacing out, the more you need a larger awareness of self to earth yourself with and the more your system will need to work to establish you as somebody to come home to, as it were.

Solar plexus people relax best by lying out in the sun, which can give the body a great deal of strength. If you love the sun, bathe in it, tune into it: you will gather a great deal of energy which can be used by the rational, intellectual, left side of the brain. Conversely, the moon can be used to evoke the powers of intuition. If we open up the intuitive right side of the brain we get a feeling of being cosmic and 'spaced out'; while if we develop the left side we grow analytical and rigid, closing everything away into neat little categories. The classic example of the two working together harmoniously is that of learning music with the left brain and enjoying it with the right; but generally the left is, as we know, at loggerheads with the right, fearing it, questioning it exhaustively and dismissing anything that lies beyond the rational and physical. This sort of thinking is extremely inhibiting to the psyche, but it can have practical advantages, as Lilla's experience in the British Museum shows.

The solar plexus is really the breakthrough chakra. Energy can be gathered here and made available in order for us to reach the higher levels of consciousness and open into wisdom. But all too often it stops short: we do not make contact with wisdom but stay with our memories, remembering and parroting ideas and thoughts, which are not wisdom at all. So evolution can only take place when this centre is connected to the soul and to the higher energies rather than sinking down towards the lower vibrations. We need to step up from the ego, the 'I' in us, and connect with the 'I AM'. As we begin to open we sometimes experience a dual personality. Here a person seems to be split down the middle: part of him appears very spiritual and part of him absolutely beastly. This is why energy has to be purified, raised and constantly balanced.

There is all the difference in the world between turning this area into golden wisdom and using it in the self-centred pursuit of pleasure and personal gain. Competition and ambition in all fields of life affect the soul and make it impossible for the centres to function in a spiritual way. If

65

you develop your solar plexus, you can certainly become a powerful individual: you can have a brilliant mind, acquire a great deal of money and material goods; you can become hypnotic, you can mesmerise people and be so magnetic that they will worship you. But if you awaken the solar plexus without understanding what you are doing, your body will take over and you will become a slave to its desires.

Overcharging the solar plexus will affect both chakras on either side: the abdomen and the heart. Not only will the digestion and assimilation be affected but there will also be a tendency to become insecure and overassertive; to be competitive, wanting to be the centre of any scenario or conversation. You will suffer from a lack of compassion and understanding (although you may be sentimental). You will get easily upset if what you want fails to materialise, and will feel that you are not being taken seriously. As soon as the solar plexus becomes overcharged, the left side of the brain becomes overactive and the person in question becomes self-centred, geared to his own survival and to helping himself rather than others. Relationships will be approached in a logical way with himself in view: people will be used for what can be got out of them in the way of money, brain, sex, physical effort, and so on. Many of us live with another person for purely materialistic reasons of security: for example, a woman who does not want to fend for herself will be quite willing to have a little sex and be married in order to be comfortable (although women in whom this chakra is overcharged will often be more interested in having a career than children).

Insecurity

Our competitive urban environment may be safer and more substantial than a jungle, but it brings with it its own brand of insecurity. Will we lose our job? Our income? Our lover, wife or husband to our friends and neighbours? Insecurity is a craving to be noticed by others, and it probably starts with conditioning right at the beginning of life. We feel we are nobody and so put everything we have into proving we can achieve something. Insecurity tends to make us talk a lot

66

about ourselves and have little time for others, unless they happen to fall into the category of lover, friend or business associate and so be directly associated with our own lives and desires. There is often an overwhelming need to get people, particularly our children, to do what we want. And overall there is the question: 'What will happen to me?' There is the need to have this and that, to amass possessions in order to create some semblance of security.

The worship of gold

The acquisition of gold has always made people important in some way. Man has always had to amass material goods so as to demonstrate power. In the temples, as the real powers declined and vibrations became lower, initiates took to wearing more and more gold in order to make up for the loss of energy within themselves. Gradually it became a widespread desire to adorn the body with gold: to dress sumptuously and become opulent by surrounding oneself with treasures, thereby obtaining power through possessions.

Once a person has developed certain levels there is no doubt that it is possible for him to manipulate matter to create and amass gold. There have been people who were capable of taking base metals and changing them to gold on physical levels. The Leopold-Hoffman medal, still in possession of the family, is the most outstanding example of the transmutation of metals ever recorded: two-thirds of it was transformed into gold by the monk Wenzel Seiler, a third of it remaining in its original silver. The enigmatic Comte de Saint-Germain was a famous adept of the time of Louis XV, and his powers were extraordinary. Saint-Germain was a brilliant painter, musician, chemist and linguist, fluent in German, English, Italian, Portuguese, Spanish, French, Greek, Latin, Sanskrit, Arabic and Chinese. His magnificent and mysterious collection of paintings, precious stones and elixirs was renowned and vanished completely on his death, which was equally mysterious, if not quite as magnificent. Casanova[31] records an occasion when Saint-Germain changed a twelve-sol piece into a pure gold coin; however, Casanova was something of a doubting Thomas and intimated to Saint-Germain that he was sure another coin had been substituted. Saint-Germain was not pleased. 'Those who are capable of entertaining doubts of my work are not worthy to speak to me!' he thundered. Casanova was shown out and never saw him again. Another instance was witnessed by the Marquis de Valbelle when he visited Saint-Germain in his laboratory and found the alchemist busy with his furnaces.

> He asked the Marquis for a silver six-franc piece and, covering it with a black substance, exposed it to the heat of a small flame or furnace. M. de Valbelle saw the coin change colour until it turned a bright red. Some minutes after, when it had cooled a little, the adept took it out of the cooling vessel and returned it to the Marquis. The piece was no longer of silver but of the purest gold. Transmutation had been complete. The Comtesse d'Adhémar had possession of this coin until 1786 when it was stolen from her secretary.[32]

Saint-Germain, as Manly P. Hall tells us in his introduction to *The Most Holy Trinosophia*,[33] was one of those whose words and actions demonstrate clearly that they are of an order different from the rest of society – and it is interesting to note that the principles he disseminated were permeated with Gnostic doctrines. At various times he himself admitted that he was obeying the orders of a power higher and greater than himself. But most people, if they amass material riches, are generally pulled down by the forces of gravity.

The whole point of alchemy was to teach us to transform ourselves to gold within the chakra system, to turn all the centres to gold. All initiates worked to obtain a gold halo of energy and gold in all the chakras. When we get the golden vibration strongly, we, like King Midas, turn everything to gold. The gold vibration is very cleansing, and there is a tendency for rich men and women to collect beautiful things, works of art, fine furniture and paintings – things that vibrate well. They often collect and wear gold, silver and precious stones, all of which have a purifying and revitalising effect. As they get older they need the energies of silver, gold and gemstones more and more as their auric space deteriorates. It is worth mentioning here that gold is often used in the packaging of items that are harmful: cigarettes, alcohol and chocolates, for example.

Fear

Whenever primitive man was in danger he had either to run away or fight. Fear engenders the energy needed for something to happen. There is a great collection of nerve endings in the solar plexus, and in a state of fear or shock the chakras flash into motion, exercising the feet and hands; the mouth opens, and all the muscles of the ear come into play. But if we have nothing specific to do with the energy we will have difficulty in controlling it. Many of our everyday modern pursuits bring turmoil for which there seems to be no appropriate outlet. Driving is a well-known cause of increased agitation. Similarly, if we wait at a bus stop feeling furious that the bus is late, we produce a great deal of energy; yet all we can do is stand there seething. This undercurrent of tension and frustration contains nothing tangible either to fight or run away from, and the result is widespread digestive and heart disorder.

Ironically, many of our current problems are created by ourselves. In our modern tame society we rarely suffer from dangerous confrontations. Many people feel boredom, a lack of excitement; they long for the flow of adrenalin and so go out in search of kicks. Some resort to climbing rocks and mountains, to potholing, driving fast cars and motor bikes, flying aeroplanes – even to dabbling in the occult. Others charge their centres in more vicarious ways. If you look at sexy films or books this will titillate the base chakras; wars and westerns excite the abdomen, which responds also to sport. The solar plexus is stimulated by horror films and tales of suspense and detection, and, judging by the current boom in the horror-video and crime-fiction industries, many of us are busy stimulating this particular area. What can happen is that a person may be so highly stimulated by what he sees on television or reads that he will be scared to go out. Moreover, by creating thought-forms on the etheric he can draw to himself physically those things that frighten him most.

Nowadays minds are churning, adrenalin is flowing, the solar plexus is gathering energy, and people are producing all kinds of uneasiness and anxiety which they find difficult to control. Often what happens is that the gathering of force in the solar plexus connects us with some deep-rooted problem. We all conceal inner dreads, which drink, cigarettes, sedatives and other people may help to cushion, enabling us to relax. But we must try to face up to our fears and see them in a different light; we have to fight and overcome the dragons in our lives. If, for example, we are afraid of speaking in public and find ourselves unable to mask this fear, our psyche will never progress. What many of us fail to realise is that when we are frightened of something and worry away at it we give that fear resolution and it is likely to grow bigger. It is therefore important to try to get to the root of our horrors. All fears are the components of growth; we should not only learn from them but also grow through them, grow in our understanding not only of ourselves but of others.

Phobias

At the root of all phobias lies the fear of death. As soon as we see something that upsets us we produce adrenalin and gather the energy to fight or run away. Phobias are, in the first place, only triggers for releasing that mechanism. The classic fears are of spiders, mice – tiny things. Common sense tells us we should not be running away, yet all that energy builds up inside us – and there we are. We are unable to fight it: it is too small and we are unable to attack it psychically because we do not know how to. The result is that we become terrified and rooted to the spot. Meanwhile the gathering of this enormous energy causes symptoms and eruptions: a flow of adrenalin, a thudding heart, a terrible feeling in the stomach. What happens is that we are fighting not so much the spider or the mouse as our own energies. All these feelings are being produced because of our inaction, and we remain stuck there while all that energy builds up. Now, the sensible thing is to use that energy in a constructive way. First of all, it is important to be the witness, the watcher: so many people

70

are unable to look at the state they are in – they *are* that state. If we get to the point of creating and gathering energy and of feeling inexplicably uneasy, then we need to observe, to say to ourselves: 'I've got this energy: what I need to do is programme it in a practical, left-brained way, see what its workload is.' What we need is control: lack of control allows energies to mount up until they become too strong for us to cope with.

There is nothing new in suggesting that the roots of many of our deeper problems can be traced back to a period in our lives which appears to have been forgotten. Sometimes they can be traced back to childhood; sometimes to past lives. People who have a tendency to gather energy and overcharge the solar plexus may be closely linked to past fears. The solar plexus holds with it all memories of our evolution and past lives, and under hypnosis and regression we can gain access to these deeper memories. Sometimes we need to go deeper into energies in order to understand them and their cause. We have only to look at history to see the wide selection of horrible experiences that are available: torture, starvation, incarceration, burning at the stake, and so on. It was not uncommon to be buried alive. People were sometimes interred with their husbands and masters: if a man was rich and powerful, it was the custom for his wives and servants to be entombed with him. On a more mundane note, medical diagnosis was not always reliable, so that a person might have been pronounced dead when merely unconscious. The shock of the earth being shovelled in on top of him could have started him breathing again, while at the same time he might have begun to suffocate and eventually to choke to death. Another awful fate was to be left semiconscious to be eaten alive by vultures or maggots.

The antidote to all these horrors is first of all to try to understand them and then to programme yourself so that this uncontrollable energy is not produced. It is helpful to release fears through regression, meditation and relaxation: to bring them up to the surface and observe them in the light of common sense, which will help to dispel them. Just thinking about fear may cause symptoms, and breathing quickly is one of these. The solar plexus will immediately react to fast breathing, releasing more adrenalin and more energy; so you must relax, breathe well and challenge the symptoms. When you are able to control your breathing you will never fall apart. Whatever the phobia, sit down and breathe into it, and eventually the breathing will conquer. Of course, fears that have built up over many years – many lives even – are deeply established, and dealing with them is not easy. So we must have patience and perseverance. Many people confirm that after a year or so of breathing exercises and of controlling their physical bodies through yoga or some other form of exercise their phobias disappear.

Basically, the solar plexus is there for our protection, but in imaginative individuals it can have the opposite capacity: the more creative you are and the stronger your imagination, the greater will be your ability to create enormous thought-forms. Ironically, what often frightens people are the monsters they themselves have created, the thought-forms they have impressed on the etheric. Through their imagination their problems can be hugely magnified. The ability to magnify is one of the psyche's most precious tools, but if uncontrolled it can work against us, causing a tiny spider to become twenty, thirty times larger, as big as a house, or a small negative idea something we cannot possibly cope with.

A fear of heights is something else again, and often derives from changes in energy fields. Energy rushes to the top of the head, and you feel top-heavy and dizzy. In this case you need to earth yourself – you need more energy in your feet – and you do this by drawing the attention down to the soles of the feet. Open countryside can also affect energies: chakras may start to quicken, and the 'spaced-out' feeling this causes can become terrifying. Again, the antidote is to earth oneself and use the heavy gravitational forces to pull one's energies down into the feet.

Drugs

Drugs either result in an under or overcharging of this area, depending on which kind of drug is used. When our fears become too much for us and make us unable to sleep, relax or concentrate, we hurry off to the doctor and get prescribed bottles of tranquillisers and/or sedatives which lower the charges of energy, slow down the centres and suppress our symptoms. It is possible to see the solar plexus actually slowing down under the influence of these drugs, which kill off the natural ability to attract energy to this area so that fears are subdued. The ability to sense becomes numbed; indeed, it is impossible to sense consciously what is going on at all. People who are on these types of relaxing drugs barely seem to move in the solar plexus.

Hallucinogenic drugs, on the other hand, are one of the most common causes nowadays of this centre becoming overcharged. In this case, adrenalin will be flowing all the time and the person in question will find it difficult, almost impossible, to be calm and still. At first these drugs seem to make this centre develop beautifully and become large and active; but after a while the centres on either side of it begin to distort and crack and the system experiences symptoms of overcharging. Another problem is that through taking too many drugs a person loses his awareness of spirit: in other words, he becomes dependent on the drugs to put him in touch with his spirit. Narcotics can certainly raise our energies, but (and this is why cleansing is so vital) if our centres are not clean we will be sending impurities – negative energies – into the brain. In the temples, as we know, drugs were often administered in a strictly controlled environment so that initiates could boost their energies and get a glimpse of the states they were working to achieve; once they had seen their potential they had to work hard to get there under their own steam.

Schizophrenia

Schizophrenia is a classic case of this area overcharging. The first thing a schizophrenic should do is contact a dowser or a practitioner of radionics – somebody able to discover in what his system is deficient. A lack of vital vitamins, trace elements or minerals can cause a debilitating imbalance, since the organs will not be capable of operating correctly; certain vitamins, particularly vitamin B, may be burning up. So schizophrenics need to look closely at their diet and

73

probably to supplement it. Usually they are clever people but unable to talk too well about their own experiences, and they know so much conflict, so much inner turmoil, that their minds go round in circles and they get yet more debilitated. The black hole opens up to gather energy, which makes them more overcharged than ever: egocentric and demanding. They grow increasingly selfish, self-centred, their will completely tied to their bodily functions. Ideally, they need to try to work hard: preferably at something of benefit to mankind and preferably at something physical that will use up the energy as opposed to suppressing it by the use of pills, which will make them too sluggish and sleepy to do anything physical. Painting, making things with the hands, working in the open air are good ways for such people to release energies. They need to be surrounded by a supportive and uplifting atmosphere, by beautiful music, and, if they are able to concentrate, by inspiring books. They need a lot of nature in their environment and need to learn, through meditation, how to control their energies rather than making them stronger; how to channel them, control them and close them down. They need to have their past cleared out and, above all, they need to understand themselves.

Suggested ways of improving the solar plexus

For our solar plexus to work efficiently we have to be well balanced, and to achieve this we need to be supple and active, with good circulation, which also benefits the heart. Then to be able to use the solar plexus for our growth we need to do certain things. We need to stop thoughts from coming into our minds without permission; to concentrate on and give our attention to whatever we set out to do. If we have a solar plexus that is not working properly, we need to cleanse and purify it. First it should be relaxed; then emptied. This is a discipline in itself, an opening kind of discipline which should be understood as a letting go. We must develop the ability to let go very deeply, so first we have to sense what it is that we are letting go. The key to this is clarification: we have to sit quietly and look. Initially we must deal with our fears, to recognise those phantoms which have haunted us all our lives; we must recognise them and let them go. It is therefore a good idea to list the fears, to observe the patterns of life, the failures, the pain, the setbacks, the difficulties.

The most effective method, as we know, is that which leads us to put our problems clearly to ourselves so that we ourselves may find the answers. We have to set ourselves examination papers, as it were, so we need to know the proper questions to ask. It is useful to prepare the ground by clarifying. Look at your habits, likes and dislikes, prejudices, opinions and judgements. Look at the amount of vital energy that goes into unnecessary preoccupations, actions and talk. See clearly what has been impressed upon you by conditioning and convention, family, culture and country. Stand in front of a mirror and look carefully: who is that person, really, looking at you? Look carefully at the reflection and the effect of light and shadow. How much are you in light, and how much darkness? What are you doing? What are you seeking? What are your motives? What is your attitude? What is your aim?

The solar plexus is the centre for looking and examining, for accuracy and precision, the vital centre for sensing. Sit, for example, with an apple and try to understand, to sense and feel the tree, the leaf, the branch, the roots and, through the roots, the earth. Sit with a flower and do the same thing: watch a flower open just as it needs the sun; watch its desire. Now watch that within yourself which is seeking the light and sense the reverberation of this vital force. Look again at yourself. How does the floor feel under your feet, for instance? How does the grass feel? What are you perceiving? How much energy are you giving out and how much of it are you wasting? How much more energy could you use, and are you able to get it if you need it? Are you concentrating too much on yourself? Sense the geometry of your body, your inner and outer space; sense every texture and sound in the room and know how it affects you. What is your body telling you? Pay attention to every detail of your life. It is a good policy to do as the monks of former times used to do and, every night before going to sleep, review the day that is over and see how you have dealt with your time and energy.

This is the centre of concentration, of building and constructing, the centre for shaping inner knowledge – the centre of sacred geometry. The concept of the ancients was that we are created out of patterns that can be represented in the architecture of temples, cathedrals and churches. Here is extended, external body awareness, one might say, for such sacred buildings are archetypes representing that which the master builders were trying to create within themselves. Ancient exercises for controlling the solar plexus included the creation of structures with the mind. Each structure you make, whether a dot, a circle, a square or triangle, can be a key. This is because there is a geometry in all created things which is made out of force lines coming together at various angles, and what you are really doing is making the idea of the basic universal structure larger so you can tune into it. You can sit inside a real pyramid, make one with a few sticks, or create one in the mind with the breath – it does not need to be solid; just the outline of its structure can work on the consciousness and link it to creative levels, those basic levels from which the universe was formed. A good exercise is to concentrate first on a triangle, then on a square, then on a circle, and notice the difference in energy.

Breathing exercises for the solar plexus

It is particularly important when working on the solar plexus to be balanced and centred in the auric space. Breathing properly with a good, long out-breath releases and relaxes much tension here. The exercise for breathing round the aura is especially good for the solar plexus. So breathe around your body in an oval shape from right to left seven times, then seven times up the back and down the front. Never do these more than seven times. Play around with the exercise, though; experiment at making the primordial oval shape bigger and bigger. Sense beyond yourself. Then tune into the middle of your body and you will feel that it has changed in some way; while on the outside, too, things will feel different. Next, try surrounding yourself with a circle, a square and a pyramid: you do this in the same way, by breathing round the body in the shape with which you are working. Again never more than seven times.

It is by gaining a true understanding of someone or something on telepathic levels that we shall help to unite the world. We all know how difficult it can be to get a person to understand a point of view that is new or foreign to him. Indeed, once a human being gets set in his ways, it becomes very difficult to establish communication with him on any level at all, he is so embedded in all the things he has built around him as protection. Telepathic communication requires no language; it is pure feeling and sensing; an exchange of vibrations playing backwards and forwards. Using this sort of reciprocation we can discover precisely what someone or something really is, from the size and shape to the essence. Communication can be established on really deep levels.

Exercise for sensing and exchanging energies

Imagine you have a large, round object like a ball. First use your hands as antennae, feeling round it gently. Next forget the hands and top part of the body and think only of your feet. Move your feet over and round your object and sense its shape with your feet, which know exactly what the object is like. Compare this information with that which was received by your hands. Next, imagine that your hands and feet have grown into your body and that you are having to sense the ball with the whole of your torso. Try to feel it, back, sides and front, and keep your awareness touching it. If the ball floats, keep bouncing it. Try to feel it move; feel it as a weight, as it balances, so that you really get to the point where the object is alive. Now try to sense the ball with your hands, your feet and the whole of your body all at the same time. This means that if the ball is floating in water it no longer matters whether it is down by your feet, near your hands or close to your head. Every part of the body knows how far away it is, where it is and what is happening to it. You sense the ball right through the body, and your eyes are no longer necessary. What is really happening is that you are sending out sounds through the body so that they keep touching the ball; the ball emits sound in its turn, and every time a different part of the body touches it, that sound alters slightly.

Next, imagine that you are standing in the middle of a room

blindfold and that you pick some small object and start to project energy on to it. When you have finished, select a larger object and do the same thing. Notice that with the big object your energy patterns open up into a large beam but that with the small one the beam is more condensed, more intense. In this way you will be able to exchange energies with objects and become able to examine them. Now, think of what is behind you and what is on either side. Realise that out of your whole body consciousness there radiates a certain band of sound. Imagine you are standing there and that all around you are sounds. Sense what is behind, what is to the left and to the right. You do this by sending out waves of energy, just as the waves of the sea send out waves of energy. So imagine waves of energy streaming out from you, working either to open or to condense, so that you are able to sense the object you are exploring through every hair and pore in your body. Remember that the object will not merely lie flat but have depth, breadth and length, so move around it and bathe it in the sound you are sending out until you can feel it from every angle. You will be able to send out your beams to one side of the room and sense all the dimensions of your object, at the same time feeling something on completely the other side of the room. For example, in the case of driving a car you eventually become able to do this automatically so that you are capable of thinking about other things at the same time.

CHAPTER FIVE
The Heart

With the heart, we are once again group-oriented. We are part of everything at both ends, as it were, only coming in at the solar plexus to the idea of individuality. The idea of being an individual and at the same time part of a group, a collective consciousness, can be illustrated by the following example. Imagine three people sitting in a room. They are all individuals, yet if you think of them as torches they are capable of putting their light together to make one large beam. In the same way, when twenty people in a room are full of light they will create an enormous beam, an enormous field of light; yet they will still retain their individuality. So we can be separate and at the same time be one with a collective consciousness. Paradoxically, we lose nothing of ourselves while losing everything. We evolve and grow individually, yet we can feel the fire of others and become part of that fire. Like a beautiful lawn in summer each blade of grass is separate yet so close to all the rest that they glitter together under the sun. Each of us is an individual spark of energy, and what happens when two energies meet and a real exchange takes place is an explosion. It may be small or large and it may manifest on different levels from a sexual flame to a flash of insight or intuition.

Love is the most important commandment of all, and through true unconditional love it is possible to find peace. Yet both peace and love are qualities that, on the whole, seem wanting in our modern society. The true feelings of the heart often appear to have been bypassed and we have large doses of sentimentality instead – the sort of stuff that, for instance, allows the British attitude to animals: on the one hand, we are a nation of 'pet'-lovers with a Royal Society for the Prevention of Cruelty to Animals and so on, and on the other, we turn a blind eye to the merciless conditions of large-scale factory farming (to say nothing of the low quality, tasteless food it produces). In short, 'heartless' and 'hard-hearted' are terms which accurately describe much that is in evidence today; 'warm-hearted' and 'whole-hearted' seem somewhat rarer attributes. Yet the bigger and the warmer our hearts, the stronger we are; and love itself is a most powerful force, capable of both balancing and neutralising. Unless we are able to love and to be in harmony with a person we cannot really reach him or exchange energy with him in a real way; we will establish with him only the most superficial kind of communication. The left and right sides of the brain should be in harmony here within the heart; there should be a balance of wise and intuitive love linked closely to the will and imagination. Unless we 'put our hearts' into something – in other words unless we commit ourselves – we will really get nowhere.

Love for human beings, animals and nature is contained in the heart. Here is the natural instinct to heal and preserve rather than destroy. When we are able to open our hearts and work with animals and plants a great deal of energy flows from our hands. During a healing session, for example, the chakras in the healer's hands start to whirl and vibrate faster: yet the tips of the fingers and toes are the only places where this whirl, this whorl, is clearly visible, manifesting on the skin at the physical level. Much of this energy is the same green vibratory rate of plants: aromatherapy, herbal medicines and massage are all ways of channelling the green vibratory heart rate through the hands to help others.

The heart has a specific mission: to keep the whole system alive. But it is essential that it should be able to relax and release, for unless it is able to do so it will destroy. Athletes can develop problems here if they do not understand how to open their centres; they can overcharge their hearts and cause havoc with the energy patterns. Drugs, modern medicines, broken love affairs – broken hearts, in other words – all cause problems by breaking up the geometrical patterns of the etheric energies, and as soon as these become unable to align well the physical heart will be affected. People who work against this area and disrupt it are those who are impatient and who take on too much work and too many hobbies: their natural intuition and protective energies vanish in the hustle and bustle of their lives. The plight of the businessman is well known: excessive amounts of food and drink, a busy mind, tension in the neck and shoulders, a preoccupation with money – all these things cause marks and disruptions in the energy patterns. Instead of lifting up their hearts, businessmen often do the opposite: they allow their hearts to sink under the force of gravity. Thus their lives are usually shortened and they pay the penalty by not being able to enjoy the wealth and possessions they have accumulated. Heart attacks are more prevalent in our society than cancer. This is because of disrupted energy patterns caused by pressures of our economic climate.

There is no doubt that the heart is adversely affected by materialistic values. We know that when the solar plexus is overcharged the mind is continually preoccupied and unable to rest; and if the abdomen is also overcharged by business lunches, rich food, alcohol and tense discussions there will be a number of strong charges below the heart. If we talk a lot, attend meetings and project our voices in order to persuade people to buy from us or we manipulate them in other ways, we will be overcharging the throat centre. So our hearts, trapped between overactive centres, are quite unable to be calm and become, instead, the focus of energies that are too strong. Smoking and eating and drinking too much are all mirrored in the heart: the energies become ruined through pressure, and eventually the heart muscle will be affected and brown marks similar to burns will show up on the etheric. So the heart reflects everything we do. It is the first centre to degenerate through the effects of drugs, cigarettes and bereavement. In highly sensitive individuals it reacts to coffee and is even vulnerable to posture: it can be endangered by our way of sitting or of holding things. How do you hold your pen, for example? Or your book, your car wheel, your telephone or musical instrument? You may grip too tightly and spoil your energies. Often the heart retains negativity that is rooted in childhood: the attitude of unloving, uncaring and domineering parents may produce an equally warped and heartless individual whose only release is, as we have seen, through someone pure.

It is worth mentioning here that this centre is particularly vulnerable in healers, who, if unable to open properly, may find themselves at risk from heart attacks. A significant case of this is Madame Kulagina, one of Russia's most famous parapsychologists and, like Madame Kirlian, a victim of science. The catalogue of Madame Kulagina's abilities is extraordinary.[34] In her capacity as healer she has closed open wounds and moved partially paralysed men to walk again. She has stopped the heart of a frog, made smoke swirl inside a glass ball, and levitated matches, cigarette cases, fountain pens and other objects, through the power of her mind. Merely by looking at an envelope containing undeveloped film and by using her mind as a laser beam she has marked crosses on the film that were clearly visible when it was developed. Before beginning her experiments she would experience a sharp pain, a current of electricity or wave of heat rising up her spine, and a blurring of vision. During these experiments her heartbeat increased measurably, rising to 160, and several times she became unconscious. Sometimes after the experiments an electrical force rushed back into her body, usually through her hands and arms, leaving burns on her skin. On several occasions her clothes actually caught fire and she became so ill that her assistants had difficulty in reviving her. She endured pain, long periods of dizziness, weight loss and lasting discomfort, until finally she suffered a massive heart attack and is now obliged to lead the life of an invalid.

Falling in love

As we all know, falling in love is a marvellous experience in which we become alive and aware. It is nature's way of showing us just how much potential vitality and awareness there can be. Falling in love is really looking for a balance: a longing to be complete and whole, a longing to see the male and female energies balancing inside us. We each need a specific kind of energy in order to work at our best and feel complete. The outer need is there because we experience a lack in ourselves. Any attraction we feel to others will always be in order to complete ourselves. The problem with an unhappy love affair is that because our femininity or masculinity has been rejected, we ourselves will sometimes reject that side of our nature: the pain may make us release too strongly into the opposite.

When someone touches us, the messages received are usually sensual. Yet making love is really the balancing of the chakras: two people trying to create light together, to go beyond the head, beyond the laws of gravity. Ideally, both should be linked with all the bodies, the etheric, the astral and the mental; there should be a merging of being. Love on the purely physical level is only a fraction of the real experience and ends up being unfulfilling. When a relationship is based on wisdom and intuition rather than sex urges the result is a union in which both can feed each other with productive ideas and give each other energy and support. The whole point of a relationship is to make the couple creative; the whole point of two people being together is that they should complement each other. If the sex, the ideas, the meals they share, are not inventive, if the conversation between them is not stimulating and their hearts are not resounding, then the couple are not growing enough. We should not be trying to possess our partners, to manipulate and hold on to them; what really matters is how the relationship balances so that harmony may be created. Both harmony and disharmony can be inherited. A child growing up in an unharmonious environment can, when married, pass on disharmony to his own child. What happens is that members of families down the generations bequeath an interweaving of vibrations through the system of cords which bind them together. All this negative inherited material continues to be handed down through ignorance of what is actually happening.

The process of a relationship is either to open our hearts to everything and engender enormous feelings of freedom, beauty and love or to make us crucify ourselves, which again means opening our hearts, but this time through pain. Great joy and great pain: both can awaken us. The mistake is to close ourselves down when we have unpleasant experiences. Pain is for learning from, and our attitude towards any sort of suffering is crucial: if we spend our lives complaining, our centres will get worse rather than better. So we should accept and learn from our suffering. We will understand others better if we ourselves have been ill, divorced, insane – how can we help others if we have absolutely no experience? We must grow and mature through our mistakes.

Often we enter into a relationship and create a marvellous feeling of love and the heart starts to expand. Then that relationship breaks up. We have grown accustomed to having that person around, accustomed to the energies going up the spine – and suddenly the cords are cut. All that energy hangs about getting darker and darker; yet it is still there for us to use and the secret is to transmute it. If you find it difficult to raise yourself up after a love affair has gone wrong, then it is better to use that energy for something else: sport, studying, music, gardening, helping other people. The antidote is always to use the energy in a constructive way, preferably working with and helping others. If you have had a lot of unhappy love affairs in your life with people who seemed wrong for you, this means you have been given certain lessons to learn. As we progress through life we often fall in love more than once and face certain scenarios again and again. Love is a vibration, and sometimes we can find quite a lot of people whose vibrations are similar to those of someone we loved in a past life. Something about the way they look, smile, walk, talk, or feel, will remind us on a deep level that there was once something like this, something so attractive – and then we fall in love again.

Through the whole of our lives we may meet people, fall in love with them, live with them, yet there is a feeling that none of them *understand*. Our understanding of others is linked to our relationship with ourselves. This is really what we have to sort out. The challenge is to be able to get together with another on such a level that we become able to understand that person completely. Once we can do this, we will no longer need our partner for mundane reasons. Once we have reached a complete understanding of another person we will understand humanity and we will understand ourselves; to put it another way, we can find universality by searching either within ourselves or within others. Most of us certainly find it difficult, impossible, to love everybody – all the neurotic people as well as the easy ones – for there is always something to work out. Yet it is up to us to measure how much we can grow through others, not just through those we love but also all the rest. It is when we find forgiveness with the people who are close to us that we will really gain spiritually. It is very often the ones we are closest to with whom we are required to succeed: our mothers, fathers, sisters, brothers, children, lovers, the people we marry. These have all been sent to try us and are really the biggest challenge of our lives: if we run away from them, we will never make them love us deeply and our hearts will never become clean and beautiful. Each relationship should make us grow; but each time we allow ourselves to forget it is with that mysterious power called God we really seek a relationship, we stunt our growth.

Strokes and epileptic fits

Strokes usually occur when there is no energy flowing etherically, that is to say when there is a blockage of energy in the etheric body with no energy coming from the feet. Very often the same is true of epileptics, except that their energy goes up either the left or the right side of the spine as opposed to the centre. Just before a stroke occurs the energies in the second nervous system will start to block and there will be no energy at all in the feet. Certain signs will appear: a numbness round the heart and a pain at the back of the neck. It is important to lie down, concentrate on the feet, breathe calmly and focus on relaxing the top of the head and releasing from the hands and feet; it is probably better not to eat for the rest of the day. It is as if the spirit is trapped in the body and unable to release its mechanism and so loses contact with the other bodies. If you are prone either to epileptic fits or strokes you need to work hard at relaxation in order to control your body and mind, to eat all the right foods and be aware of any signs that might manifest.

Suggestions for improving the heart

The heart is the centre of dissolving into the collective consciousness, into oneness and harmony. It is not only concentrating and looking at a flower, it is *being* the flower: falling in love with the flower and dissolving into it. It is caring for things that are not directly concerned with ourselves: other countries, other people's children. It is sharing ideas, possessions and energies. Listen well to the heart. It is rare that we tune into our hearts, and when our hearts tune into us, when they beat fast, pound in our ears and so on, it usually makes us apprehensive. So tune into the heart and listen to its beat. Try to open it up to love. Try to sense a way of cleansing this area. The heart cannot open until it is pure, so first of all you must dissolve any coarse particles that may be here. Be honest with yourself: if you try to pretend that pain and negativity are not there, if you lie to yourself and bottle things up, it will cause enormous problems. Imagine someone walking into a room and spilling milk on the floor, then turning his back on the spilt milk rather than dealing with it: the whole room will end up smelling bad, and the stain will get worse and worse. So it is with negativity in the heart. We have to find ways of making the cleansing real. One person imagined he had performed an operation on himself, that he had opened up his heart and let all the negativity pour out of it; another envisaged that he was vomiting up his negativity. The important thing is to make what you do essential to the mind.

Through the lungs the heart is closely linked to the breath. With a good out-breath the heart can be considerably strengthened, and breathing round the aura is beneficial. So breathe in and on the outbreath relax the heart, and here it may be necessary to take more than seven breaths. Relax the shoulders, the elbows and the hands; relax the face and ears. Try to soften up the neck and shoulders: unless the shoulders are in alignment and the neck is held correctly you may find it difficult to breathe and relax well. You will know when the heart is relaxed by the feeling of peace that spreads through your body. It is helpful to stretch well, to raise the arms to shoulder height, expanding the chest; then stretching them well above the head, also clenching the hands tightly and letting them go several times, sighing on the out-breath is beneficial, and so is yawning. Crying, whether in adults or children, should never be suppressed and should be allowed to continue until the release it brings about is completed. Try to think of nature and all the green colours balancing you. Relax deeply into the feeling of green, and you will find this very healthy.

Breathing and exchanging energy in the heart

To be able to use the breath completely depends on one's ability to concentrate, so concentrate well on each breath. Say to yourself: 'This breath is going to make me into what I need to be.' Follow the breath: it has to enter the lungs, and an exchange has to take place. The red blood cells carry the oxygen through the blood, so that the whole body breathes, the breath is actually contained in every single cell of the body. So sense the breath and let each inspiration reach into the deepest, most spiritual level, the I AM. Breathe for the heart, and expand and develop the feeling of love. If you do this well, you will actually be breathing out radiance and love. If you breathe consciously and your body relaxes into the feeling of love, then, with each breath, you will become more beautiful.

Imagine now that you are standing in front of yourself. Imagine that you see another you standing there. Try to feel what this other you is receiving from you in your out-breath, and try to feel that this other you is accepting it all because it feels that there is a great link between the two of you. Now imagine another human being, irritable and angry, in front of you, and immediately the quality of your breath will change and your attitude will probably reflect revulsion. So our space around us, to which we are so vulnerable, depends upon what we are, how we are and largely upon our out-breath. So sit quietly and watch the ebb and flow of your breath; see it as a body support, moving into a force for transcendence within yourself. We each have to find a way of breathing in and out which will eventually fill the room with beauty and love.

Meditation and relaxation for the heart

Make yourself very comfortable. Begin the exercise by allowing a sense of earthing. Think of browns, oranges and reds: warm colours which will earth you and make you feel comfortable and secure. Relax the feet and toes, and allow the mind to feel a deep sense of letting go and forgetting. Try to have no memories. Forget about the idea of walking, forget about paths and roads: you have only an inner path, an inner road. Relax the arms; allow them to rest. The hands have no memories of holding. You are now at another level, one where you no longer need your physical hands; so rest them and rest the shoulders. Try to look into the body, releasing the tension there so that the organs are bathed in love and light. Go into the lungs and try to feel the breath of all things; you can feel your own breath, you can also feel that the whole of the universe is breath. Every cell in your body feels safe, strong and unafraid. Imagine that though you are still sitting there you are moving from one level of awareness to another. There is nothing to tie you to any one level; you exist on all levels simultaneously.

Imagine now that you are standing in a corridor. At the end of it is a light, and as you go towards the light you feel a strange and beautiful feeling of opening out. The air vibrates more and more so that the vibrations within you feel lighter and higher. Your feet feel a path, and as you go down this you feel a garden expanding in front of you, the trees, the flowers, the lake, all shimmering in front of you. As you go up to the flowers you find they are composed of energies and that when you touch them your hands vibrate and feel full of energy, as though a current of energy is pouring out of them. Tune into the feeling of yellow and green; tune into the feeling of the sun, the feeling of green fields. Now try to feel you are a leaf; try to feel what the underside of a leaf feels like. Try to feel the various cell structures and try to sense how the sun feels. Imagine the leaves radiating blue and green vibrations which flow into you. Just relax and feel these for a little while; then try to feel how a bird feels when it sings, when it is surrounded by all these beautiful blue and green vibrations, and how it is aware of these energies. Tune into the trees deeply and drink in the green. Imagine the rings of a tree; imagine the various seasons of growth. With your imagination, try to feel that you can put your hand inside the trunk and feel the different vibrations coming from various rings, from the time when it began its life. Relax and drink in the energy.

When you are ready, look into the distance: there is a beautiful building. Feel it vibrating, shimmering, alive. As you draw near you see that it is approached by a stone avenue paved with coloured mosaic. Feel whether your feet are reaching its colours, and, as you walk down this mosaic avenue, feel whether they are picking up the vibrations. Wait at the door; then go in. Be very aware of going through this door. Imagine that just inside there is a bowl of clear water and a white robe is hanging there. Imagine that you wash yourself, then put on this clean white robe. Now walk very gently into the huge circular room. In the middle there is a great fountain of energy: sense this fountain with all its millions of tiny vibrations. Imagine now your own energy, your own aura, is like this fountain and that you can sense its movement over you, over your face, in front of and behind you. Walk towards the fountain, hold out your hands and try to gather a little of its energy. Try to sense how it feels, try to see that there are pools around it, see that it is flowing everywhere. Try to feel that you can touch it and play with it; it is everywhere. Sense that you yourself have become part of that fountain. When you feel you have done enough, go to the side of the room, sit down comfortably and try to sense any presence that is in the room. Although your eyes are closed, you can see right round the back of your head. Now try to feel that you have beside you all the people and animals who are closest to you; any person or animal who may be ill and whom you want to help; anyone you are feeling unhappy about or with whom you are having difficulties. Try to feel that they are beside you and that you are folding them into a blanket of love. When you are ready, come back into your body. Feel your toes, your hands. Just relax and enjoy the room, the peace, the place in which you are sitting – and when you are ready, open your eyes.

CHAPTER SIX
The Throat

The function of this area is twofold: to begin the process of eating and to communicate. We have in this twentieth century every facility for communication: we can lift a telephone and speak to someone on the other side of the world; we have access to every sort of newspaper, television and radio programme, radar signal and so on. Our planet is filled with the jabber of voices – yet we have lost the power of words. It is interesting here to explore briefly the nature of language, a mechanical means for composing the words in the dictionary and for transmitting the thoughts these encompass. Our words are sounds and symbols linked together which have fixed, memorised associations and which we compose in sequential patterns within the mind. In effect, then, we can understand nothing beyond that which the dictionary knows, and the contents of the dictionary is limited to definitions and notions already acquired. As soon as thought approaches the metaphysical, we no longer find in our language the means to express it. The ancient Egyptians did not use words as we do, and this is borne out by the research of Isha and René Schwaller de Lubicz.[35] Instead, for them, words were of a musical nature, a process of generating sonar fields which established an immediate vibratory identity with the essential principle that underlies any object or form. The ancients had so many incantations: words of power and ceremony. For them, words were tools.

Most people today are quite unaware of how the sound of their own name can affect them, unaware of what their name, when uttered, can do either to themselves or to others. If you say a person's name in a loving, positive way this is quite different from saying it on a low, aggressive note, which can be an extremely unpleasant experience. So just as we have to be aware of how we eat as much as what we eat, we must observe the words we say and how we say them. We must develop an awareness of sound and of words. The same word can be given a whole range of different tones. A passage intoned in the right way can raise the consciousness; but if it is given the wrong key and the wrong level, nothing will happen. Sounds can physically alter the roof of the mouth – the palate – which is one of the most important yet most neglected areas of the body, and one way of using sound is to roll it around the roof of the mouth so as to produce a vortex in order to draw up the consciousness.

Sound

Sound is not just a local experience concerning the ears but actually passes directly through the body's pores and cells. It can react variously on the consciousness and produce the ability to sense in many directions. The greatest recorded experience of all is the fall of the walls of Jericho to the sound of trumpets. Much ancient music was inspired by the sounds of nature: grass moving in the wind, ripples on the water. The development of various instruments, from the very primitive to the very complicated, came about not primarily for pleasure but in order to call people to meetings and specific ceremonies; for communication with, and adoration of, the gods rather than hobbies and pastimes. Everything and everyone – every tree, every flower, every stone – has its own particular tone which changes through the day, but we can hear only those we are capable of hearing. The more materialistic a person, the more weighed down by the forces of gravity, the lower his sound will be. Just as certain individuals are too heavy to reach some dimensions, so their sound is very low. As primitive man progressed and began to use the left side of his brain, he lost his ability to see the invisible and hear the inaudible. Hitherto, he could sense sounds rising up from the earth and from plants and trees. Some could detect sounds emanating from other planets and knew the sound of this one. These days only dogs, horses and bats hear high-frequency sounds that are unavailable to human ears, and there are on the market modern dog whistles whose sound is

91

audible only to the animals themselves. Just as the other invisible forces, like electricity, are used every day, various sounds are now known to have a wide range of uses, from killing bacteria to measuring the ocean. Ultrasonic therapy, for example, is a physical vibrating of tissues which shakes out toxic substances and helps loosen painful calcium deposits.

If you have a strong connection between the base and the top of your body, a sound can give you a climax. You can, through saying mantras, have a climax without moving – just by chanting – because you are producing certain types of energy. Just as in sexual orgasm the roof of the mouth is lifted because it is hit by a powerful energy, so certain sounds, through raising the roof of the mouth, invite more energy to go up the spine. To put it the other way round, when the body produces more energy something has to happen: we have to fight, run away, scream, sing or have a climax. Sounds have different vibratory rates. Some, when we make them, can quicken the pineal and pituitary glands, and bring the ears up and back. There are sounds for every part of the body, and, in the past, one which was capable of altering states of consciousness was considered sacred. The chants of the Gnostics are interesting here: 'Zoxathazo a ōō ēē ōōō ēēē ōōōō ēē ōōōōōōōōōōōō ōōōōō uuuuuu ōōōōōōōōōōō ōōō Zozazoth.'[36] This prayer, from the *Discourse on the Eighth and Ninth* (levels) would seem far more at home among Mongolian and Tibetan devotions than as part of orthodox Christian psalmody. The vowel sounds have always been considered holy: all five vowels increase energy supplies in the body, fill the cavity of the mouth and quicken the pituitary and pineal glands. They also work on the nerves of the third eye, the muscles of the face and those behind the ears – the ears being another neglected part of our anatomy and the cause of some modern problems. Primitive man manipulated his psyche by manipulating his ears, and animals still retain auricular mobility. If you pull your ears down you will find that the roof of your mouth will go up. Again if you chant the vowel sounds one after the other, or a traditional mantra, or the name of God, these will raise the roof of the mouth and produce changes in your consciousness. In the case of the holy sound 'AUM', the mouth is opened to its fullest extent in order to discharge the sound; the 'M' closes up the mouth again and acts as an earth. So certain sounds used in traditional mantras and Gregorian chant vibrated the roof of the mouth, drew back the ears and with their rhythmic monotony, they wove a spell. Sometimes they can produce an enormous amount of energy, enough on occasions to see the invisible, to look into the past and future and inside structures.

The point of repetitive sounds used by the Church was very definite. The rosary was not just for praying to the mother archetype, but to repeat the words over and over again so that you were brought to a state of trance so that your brainwave might change. The sound of temples, with their arches, domes, towers and spires, was one of the most important factors. A temple was only valid if it sounded right. Knowledge of sacred space has to do with creating harmony of structure and acoustics, and the ancients found that if a chant was performed by someone standing within geometrical patterns such as a stone circle or under the curve of a dome, its sound became amplified and created a rapport with the cosmos. The length and breadth of a temple, church or place of worship had to harmonise with man so that when he sang or chanted the sounds became transformed. The bigger the temple or church the better, for the more the resonance was amplified. The sound of the altar-stone was one of the keys to the temple and was selected by tapping and listening — indeed, all major stones were selected according to note and tone. Conversely, the noise of many of our tall modern buildings is extremely discordant. Many factories release an aggressive tone which disturbs the peace of the surrounding countryside and has a debilitating effect on our consciousness.

'Shitting out of the mouth'

We lose a great deal of our energy just through talking. On the whole, the less we talk about something the fewer problems we will have. If we use other methods of release, it is really not necessary to discuss things all the time. Everything we send up through the roof of the mouth to the pineal and pituitary glands has a vibration. If that vibration is very fast and beautiful, our whole life can become a meditation; if, on the other hand, it is slow and vibrates negatively, we are effectively sending 'shit' up to the roof of the mouth. Those individuals who are black at the base chakra and unable to release in the normal way, through the bowels, get to a point where they have to vomit it out of their mouths; they get rid of their negativity by spitting it out. Those who are inclined to talk in an unpleasant way usually have large amounts of black energy coming out of their mouths. Such people may have built up inside themselves a negative thought-form and talking about themselves may effect a kind of release and reduce the energy of the thought-form. If a person has a lot of unhappiness in the heart, the etheric gathers energy by darkening – we have to have energy in the heart or we would become exhausted. If the heart darkens, we tend to say nasty things all the time; what happens is that the pent-up energies springing from insecurities dating from our childhood or past lives are released. When a person with a very strong mind says something negative about another, he is able to shape a negative form of that person etherically. We know that if we vibrate sand with sound we can see it make wave-lines; and if we process the sound under a table with knots in its wood we see that these wave-lines become distorted. In the same way, sound can make distorted shapes in the etheric which can remain in the aura or the atmosphere. Even when that person gets into a good mood and tries to clear his mind, the negative patterns may recur and start to impinge on his consciousness.

If we say something nasty while holding an object in our hands, that object will become imbued with nastiness. Furthermore, the sound of our words can travel through a room impregnating all the articles in it. Imagine that you go with a friend into a room which has not been decorated for some time. It looks terrible and feels cold, and the day is rainy. You might say, 'Ugh! I don't like the look of this,' and your friend might agree. You both sit there complaining, and the next time someone goes into that room its gloom will have become magnified due to all the bad vibrations both of you

94

have put about; a place can be destroyed by the feelings of a few. It is also quite possible to pick up the sounds of those who have cried, screamed or otherwise vibrated the atoms of a room and lodged misery there.

If we empty ourselves by saying how dreadful a person is, we are not really emptying ourselves at all, we are just ruining our bodies and our circuits by taking in a great deal of low-class energy which will hit the roof of the mouth, ruin the thyroid and affect the pituitary and pineal. On the other hand, it is cleansing to do the opposite, to think and speak well of others. It is also cleansing to talk about one's problems, or those who create them, in a loving way, from the heart. One of the reasons that the Church introduced confession was not just so that people could kneel there talking about their sins but so that they could release their negativity. The way we use words can change our lives, so if we complain in a gentle, loving way the negativity often disperses fairly quickly. Whatever we speak about will affect not only the throat but all the other chakras as well – particularly the heart and the third eye.

Hypnotism and mesmerism

The voice can be used as an instrument of hypnosis. A hypnotist uses words in a soft, monotonous and repetitive way, throwing them out so that they become attached to the person under hypnosis and form a cord. This helps the chakras of the hypnotist to tune into and control the patient, whom fire will not burn, ice will not freeze and pins will not hurt. This is because the hypnotist is working with the patient's second nervous system, which is immume to pain and physical sensation and functions on higher spiritual regions. Often hypnotists are unaware of the cords they create, and, when they have finished their work, fail to remove them. The result is that the patient remains corded to and dependent on the hypnotist.

Mesmerism can also promote dependence. Many individuals locked up in asylums imagine themselves to be some important person or other: name a well-known person and there is sure to be someone either claiming to be himself or a relation. Napoleon is a familiar example: there are any number of Napoleons. Bonaparte's powers of mesmerism were so strong that he could change others to his vibration, manipulate them and do with them what he wanted. Many people with strong energies possess this ability. A certain teacher of the martial arts is able to see the coloured vibratory rates that emanate from his students and notices that many of them change to his own when they come into contact with his energy fields; in other words, they become for that moment an extension of himself. In the case of Napoleon, he needed a strong army. He himself could withstand hardship, and his men, as extensions of himself, felt strong and fearless in spite of being weak and hungry. During the Napoleonic Wars thousands of his men died in a state of exhaustion in which their wills were partially submitted to that of their leader and in which they had absorbed some of his properties. If, in another life, these souls are unable to face up to certain pressures, they may escape by imagining they are once more part of that strong energy and, this time, may believe themselves to be Napoleon himself. In a nicer vein, Moses achieved the same effect by producing a group soul for all the people of Israel so that they could strengthen one another; so if anyone who has touched on a life with Moses ever happens to get weak, he may imagine he is Moses. Many modern gurus are doing the same thing. They appear on the etheric like enormous sea anemones, with all those projections going out (actually their projections are more like little snakes than sea-anemone petals) which 'bite' into their disciples. In this way the vibrations of many disciples change to that of their guru, and unless they are deprogrammed such disciples are left with a deep impression at subconscious levels which may well up whenever that vibration is reached. In 200 years, no doubt, some people will be sitting in asylums imagining they are one or other of the more notorious gurus of today.

Shell shock

The effect of shell shock is well known. During the First World War hundreds of casualties were brought in from the trenches. The excruciating din caused by the fighting induced

96

a premature opening of the psyche which brought with it all the problems of overcharging: hallucinations, dizzy spells, difficulties with digestion and hearing, inability to concentrate. What is not generally realised is that some of the noise experienced in our everyday life can have the same effect on young children. The racket made by certain types of modern music, machinery, vacuum cleaners, mixers or jet planes can shock a small system and cause a child to open prematurely. One scientist who was working with a number of young children able, like Uri Geller, to make extraordinary things happen, such as bending spoons and making things disappear, told Lilla that they had all been involved in some sort of accident. Often when they have some learning or communication difficulty children sing repetitive little tunes. These are placebos, like thumbsucking, which can appear when pressure threatens. If you get into this kind of state, if a sound comes without permission and repeats itself – a repetitive snatch of music, a nursery rhyme, anything – you should observe it and learn to control it. If you find things coming into your mind that you are singing or humming, then you are giving life to something that has entered your consciousness without permission and you may end up being unable to switch it off.

Sound can also be used to remove negative processes. Decide that every time you feel like complaining you will either sing a certain thing, say certain words or utter a certain sound; by acting on the atmosphere in this way you will destroy the negative energy that you have caused. Laughter is very cleansing, and exercises the abdomen and throat. There are recorded cases of people curing themselves of serious diseases through laughter, by taking a course of humour and laughing at funny books and films. If you are in a bad mood and want to get out of it, a good way to do so is to clap your hands and cry 'Ha!' This is similar to 'Phat!', a Tibetan mantra which is uttered in a short explosive way (with a hard 'p') in order to dissolve thoughts and clear the atmosphere. Singing in the bath is also extremely cleansing, having something to do with acoustics, sound resonating in the steamy atmosphere.

Smoking

Smoking completely alters the atmosphere in a room. It is difficult for people who smoke to realise what happens when they do so. Every time they have a cigarette, the ether around them is changed and takes on a low grey or dingy yellow vibratory rate. With constant smoking a person's breath goes into darker and darker colours, ending up brown or black and filling a large part of the room – if it is not already contaminated. This can hang about for hours; indeed it can remain there always, depending on how polluted the lungs are. Even those who are usually unable to see the etheric may feel debilitated, be aware of the heaviness and blackness in the room and be badly affected.

Breathing

Faulty breathing is one of the problems of our civilisation. If a person's breathing is not correct, his throat will never be strong. Due to stress and tension most of us breathe out extremely badly. Many people use only one-third of their lung capacity, with the result that their etheric is not cleansed and their energy patterns are not cleared – so make sure that you breathe well.

Physical exercises for improving the throat

If you feel tense or that you are not relaxing successfully, bend your head back, then bring it up and drop it forward until the chin rests on the chest. Next turn it to the right several times or as many times as you think necessary; then repeat the exercise in the opposite direction.

Exercise for listening

Make yourself comfortable, close your eyes and relax the body. Start the exercise by imagining you are a sound, a universal sound. Start by reaching out for that sound and sensing your aura. Breathe around the aura very slowly seven times from right to left. Feel that the oval space around you is comfortable. End with the second to last oval space going round the room and the last one of all going beyond the room and outside, encompassing the garden. If you have no garden, visualise some flowers and trees on the last breath but keep it to the size of the room. Begin with the sounds, the beautiful sounds of the body itself. Listen to the heart. Listen to the ebb and flow of the lungs as you make an exchange of breath and feel if there is any tension. Listen to your heart again and release your hands, your shoulder centres, feeling the sound of your circulation. Sometimes you can feel sounds; sometimes you can actually hear them. Relax that area deeper and deeper. Try to remember that your body is used to hearing the sound of your heart; the organs are used to hearing it, the lungs are used to hearing it, and so is the brain. Go into the abdomen, listening. Each organ has a different sound, and when anything goes wrong its sound changes. Relax the organs very deeply and try to feel that the sounds are harmonious and that the heart is relaxing deeper as it feels the harmony of the sounds in the abdomen.

The mind is like a huge computer and makes sounds all the time: release it to the point where you feel a little quieter, a little more peaceful, so that you can sense quiet spaces in your mind. You have, right through the body, the ability to find silence and peace. Try to feel the silence that exists in you, in your body. Now walk out of that silence into the auric space and the sounds around you. Try to feel the room you are in. Do not allow anything to go beyond this room; stay there, be in it. Now, very gently go beyond, to the sound of the wind, of the trees. Try to listen beyond this room. You do not exist; the room does not exist beyond itself. Walk outside in your mind, and feel, sense, listen to the roots of the trees and grasses as they vibrate in the earth. Then put your ear to a tree and listen to the sound inside it as it sends out nourishment into its leaves. Try to see if you can feel the energy of the elementals and the lovely sense of each leaf having a sound; imagine what a tree feels like in summer when surrounded by the music of leaves.

The whole planet makes a sound. Try to sense around the planet many sounds: industrial sounds, peaceful sounds, the sounds of war, the different sounds that exist around the earth. Now at the level of creation itself there exists one universal sound in which all others are incorporated. Sometimes you can hear the sound that is yours, the one that is specifically good for you. Sense the peace, the quiet; try to feel that with all sound there can be total peace. No sound at all; now listen again to the sound in your aura and try to balance it so that it is neither too high nor too low. If, for example, you are a woman and have had to be very practical all your life you may need to raise your sound a little. It is your own sound through your body that keeps you alive, so try to feel the presence of the omnipotent sound and, just for a second, to experience the atom. Just allow yourself to go higher and higher, so that the sound almost takes you through the roof of your house. Then, when you are ready, come back into your body. Feel your toes and your hands and have a good stretch.

CHAPTER SEVEN

The Third Eye

The third eye is a precise and delicate instrument. An ordinary eye will give you some idea of what it is like. It resembles the physical eye, too, in its capacity to reflect illness and wisdom. When closed the energies form a protective pattern rather like a veil, an eyelid composed of seven layers, each of which penetrates the others. As a chakra opens, so a veil is dispersed, as symbolised by the dance of the seven veils. When you have the key you can gain access to what is known as the Akashic record, which contains everything that has ever existed. It is as though you can walk into a huge library and take down anything you like from its shelves. You can find anything you want in history; learn the evolution of any person, animal or object; speak any language.

However, the first thing to learn is that the process of opening this centre should be gradual. Some people awaken their third eye quickly and spontaneously while others need to relax for about an hour, using deep relaxation techniques, probably under instruction from a teacher, then very slowly the third eye may begin to open. Those who awaken the third eye too quickly may see more than they can cope with: opening without any knowledge is like sending a young child into the control room of a flying saucer and telling him to look at all the complicated gadgets and do something with them. To live in a world of cords, entities, elementals and angels is not easy and calls for adjustment, so possibly the greatest attribute of the third eye is to remain closed to excessive sensing. We must remember that at moments of heightened awareness our consciousness may become altered to a degree that can frighten us: we may, like Rachmaninov, hear sounds we are unable to dismiss, or we may be incapable of controlling our vision, become terrified by brilliant flashes of colour, or phobias we cannot shut out. We may think we are going mad. A sharp blow on the head can cause the third eye to open prematurely. Sometimes people who have been involved in a car accident suddenly find they can switch into past lives, which can lead to an identity crisis. In the past the opening of the third eye was connected with ceremonies which were sometimes frightening, sometimes painful. Each experience has left on our awareness a deep impression which can be recalled. At times individuals become disoriented and have no idea what they are doing. They have no feeling for anyone on earth because they are unable to relate either to earth energies or to their own bodies; they are like actors who have stumbled into the wrong play by mistake.

To open to different lives can prove traumatic and cause mental imbalance. We have all had bad lives in the past. History is a continual pageant of violence; we have all been cruel, and many of us have killed. If we have committed a murder, or any crime, the memory of it is still available, together with all the thoughts that accompanied that act. If we have been wounded in a past life, perhaps fatally, the memory remains and the chakra or chakras in the vicinity of the injury will malfunction.

Lilla's own experience, as her third eye was beginning to open, was that if anything excited her and gave her an extra boost of energy she would suddenly find herself precipitated into another life. At first she was quite out of control. Her way of coping was humour: she laughed and used her common sense. She would tell herself it was all hilarious and she would sit herself down, give herself a cup of coffee and earth herself by doing some boring housework. When confronted by the unknown we can either become scared and miserable or we can call upon a sense of humour to bring in the essential watcher, the essential witness. Above all, we must not be earnest, take ourselves seriously or get involved in what we are seeing and feeling. Like any computer, the third eye is capable of being switched off, and we must learn to plug into anything we want, naturally. Let us suppose you and a friend go into a crowded bar and sit down. The two of you will have your own space. You will be able to tune into and concentrate on your friend's discussion in spite of the

102

fact that all kinds of different conversations are going on at the same time; you will be able to select what you want to listen to. When the third eye opens, it is rather like watching television. You might suddenly find yourself viewing all kinds of scenes: historical, futuristic – anything. As a matter of fact, there are people who are unable to control even their own televisions. One man complained that all his troubles were due to television. It was all right, he said, when he was in England. He lived there for eight years and he was organised. He never watched the television. Now that he is at home in Ireland his children return from school and switch it on, and it is like a drug to him. He hates it, yet he can neither switch it off nor get up and leave the room. He can, he says, do nothing: his diet is all wrong, he smokes too much, and he can do nothing about it because he is disorganised by the television.

There are probably hundreds like him who never think of selecting what they look at of an evening; they switch on the set the moment they get in and remain mesmerised by it until they go to bed. So it is important to ask yourself a few questions. You should think of the third eye as being like a television set. Do you switch it on and leave it on all the time, like the Irishman? Or do you select the programmes you want to watch? You must learn to switch it off and not allow it to annoy you. The opening of the third eye is a gift which should bring with it beautiful new dimensions; rushing off to the doctor to get oneself certified is certainly not the answer.

The brain, as we know, is a vehicle through which energies pass. If we send up heavy, low-class energy, we may have problems with negativity; and if we send energy up either the left or the right of the spine we will get a lopsided view of everything. Whether we go towards the black or the white, the third eye is an instrument for observation; and we should avoid becoming involved in or addicted to what we are observing, either inside or outside ourselves. It is very often those of great intelligence but with little compassion or understanding of themselves or anyone else who become addicted. This in turn produces yet more energy; yet more sounds, hallucinations and voices. In our subconscious are all the dreams, all the negative conversations, we have ever had as well as all the good things. If our consciousness becomes overcharged, it will choose those parts that correspond to the way we are. If we are heavy and debilitated, we will sink down and dredge up all the dark matter that has been submerged.

So the ability to reach different levels of consciousness may produce all kinds of symptoms and hallucinations – even dual personalities. The most famous example of split personality is that of Jekyll and Hyde. Lilla once looked after a lady who had two voices, one male and one female, that perpetually screamed and quarrelled inside her. Such individuals have a cracked psyche: in other words, the alignment in the third eye disappears, causing the energies to tune into two lives or two internal types of thought-form which are at loggerheads with each other. Sometimes one of these personalities has no idea what the other is up to. If, instead of having a healthy geometrical pattern the energies crack and an asymmetrical form appears in which the vibrations are uncontrolled, then unnatural fears, hallucinations and mental illness ensue. We may lose our identity and think we are someone else; or we may be taken over by an entity and become possessed.

Ghosts

The ether, as we know, records every thought, feeling and event. But there is a distinct difference between an entity, an impression and a thought-form, all of which fall under the umbrella heading of ghosts. Some houses are haunted not by the dead but by thought-forms. Some of these are very old, created by strong minds, while others are more recent and wander about not yet dissolved because they have not encountered vibrations potent enough to disperse them. Some thought-forms have been partially erased: you might get one which is just a face and two hands. Alternatively, if what we are seeing is an impression which was caused by some incident strongly charged with emotion, any stimulus from us will meet with very little reaction: the apparition will pass through us or go past us, travelling on the level of the land as it lay at the time of the incident, it will perform a set routine and fade away. It may appear at a certain time, depending on the phase of the moon or the air pressure: for instance, during storms or similar atmospheric changes we can sometimes see people and buildings from another space-time.

An entity lacks a physical body but has centres of energy. If a person does not open up towards the energies above his head while on earth, or during the process of dying or just after his actual death, he will be unable to sense his future direction and sometimes a blockage will be set up. Lilla was called in to help with one lady who was causing tremendous disturbances. She would wake the occupants of the house moaning and groaning to let them know that she was lonely and miserable. What had happened was that she had arranged a date with her boyfriend, but he had been killed on his way to meet her and she was still waiting for him to arrive. An entity can, of course, be someone who has led a very wicked life; his lack of spiritual vibration made it impossible for him to move on to higher dimensions when he died. The highest beings of all are also entities, quite distinct from those poor lost souls who are unable to rise beyond earth level. Very high souls infiltrate earth levels, coming down to teach wisdom. Sometimes we hear them, sometimes we see them, sometimes we smell their fragrance: sometimes we see colours in the ethers. All entities have one thing in common: when they are around the atmosphere tends to change, often growing colder.

If you are afraid of the invisible world around you, this means you are not opening your heart and using the force of love. If on seeing a ghost you want to avoid the confrontation and run away, this means you are lacking in compassion and understanding. A ghost is someone who may not know where he is, what he is doing or where he is going. He probably needs help in order to be released from his condition, and the last thing he wants is a negative reaction from a human being. But we have to be careful because he may also want to fulfil desires he had while in his physical body; he may be hungry for material things and physical enjoyment. If he has lost contact with the highest aspect of himself, he may have an obsessive need of sex. We are here to discover our own

105

wisdom and do not want to be taken over and possessed by any entity, be it good or bad: we must be independent. So if we are contacted by an entity that is on a very low level, wanting fleshpots and sex – and the lower the entity the more he will want them – we must try to raise him up, to surround him with light and heal him. The Church has always gone on about possession and the casting out of devils and still holds services of exorcism. It may be sensible to call in professional help. There can be a span of hundreds of years of violence in an entity and to remove it may require very high and strong energy. Ethers, if very coarse, take a long time to disperse. We ourselves become vulnerable to entities when we accumulate wrong thoughts and fill our minds with such things as murder stories and obscene literature. When we listen to or hear something unpleasant or inappropriate we should take care to fill our minds with beautiful colours and spiritual thoughts.

Hearing voices

Should you go towards the black, you may occasionally hear a good voice telling you to be good; alternatively, if you go towards the white, you may hear a bad one urging you to be bad. Many of those who commit terrible crimes say they hear God advising them to do so: for instance, the 'Yorkshire Ripper', Peter Sutcliffe, thought God was guiding him to kill immoral women. It is important to remember that it is the amount of higher energy, or God, that you personally have within you that guides you, so you must think about what you are doing and what the voice is saying. The range of possibilities is enormous: what one person believes to be the higher self, or God, may be something created by the mind as a strong thought-form or idea and not necessarily the highest at all. What we must do initially is link ourselves to something we can get to grips with on a level of moral understanding. We must recognise that each of us creates his own personal God within himself: that is, that each of us has a particular feeling of God. If we are negative and psychic, we are capable of constructing a negative entity within ourselves and of reinforcing it through repetition. We can construct any kind of being at all. Sometimes this can take us over and we engage in conflict and inner battles with this thing for our creation. It is in this way that people subconsciously programme themselves. Something comes into their mind such as, 'I'm no good', 'I can't do this or that', or 'I'm a failure'. They repeat this over a number of years and eventually produce a totally negative energy which attacks them. So to all intent and purpose they are actually attacked by themselves, by the negative double they have created of themselves.

In the same way, if we programme a computer with negativity and hate, any message that comes out of it will be adversely conditioned. Suppose you have just had an unhappy love affair and are accordingly in the sort of condition to become linked to subconscious levels. If you keep repeating, 'I can't bear it'. 'I can't go on', 'I can't live without him (or her),' this will form a huge link with gravity; you will have programmed your computer for destruction by repeating such words over and over again. If you go towards very dark colours you get to the point where you are able to form a dark entity inside yourself. So since, in this sense, we are all programmers, it is essential that we should learn about ourselves and our attitudes. How much can we offer? How much of our energy can we use in different ways? There is no point in meditating, in going towards the black or the white, unless we realise that the energy we gather needs to be released constructively so that we can go through life enjoying it without unwanted voices and visions joining in.

Every time we eat we feed the body, and every time we feed the mind we either improve or lower the third-eye vibrations. The more keenly we are aware of beauty, the more beautiful our third eye will become. Eventually we should be able to use it, as the delicate and precise instrument that it is, for research purposes; we should be able to gather energy, raise the roof of our mouth, open our third eye and order our brains to project. But, like all instruments, the current has to be maintained in order to operate. When we plug in an electric drill (unless there is an electricity strike) there is every possibility that the current will remain constant; but, as we know, with a human being this is not the case. We can only maintain a working current of energy over a certain space of time, and when it runs down we need to relax and to recharge it.

Seeing the invisible

Most people, when they begin to see the invisible, do not stretch their hidden, often repressed gift; that is, they do not make the effort to focus their attention fully. Even on physical levels we can, on entering a room, choose how much we shall see. Some individuals notice very little, while others are far more attuned and aware. If we look at a flower without really seeing it or being aware of its energies it is because we are not making the necessary effort, not putting our attention into seeing around it. The requisite energy is either not being created at all or is too dim to be useful. The next point is that we have to observe images in our minds, and in the ether, in a very impartial way. We have to be objective and try not to be immersed emotionally in what we are doing. We need to be certain that we are not placing our trust in something we may feel to be very positive but which is really something negative hidden beneath a veil. For example, one man thought he was in touch with a very beautiful being; but it turned out later, when he challenged it, to be no good at all. When the solar plexus produces in you a large ego, you are sometimes able to see light and all kinds of wonderful things; yet these marvels are created by your own ego, by your own imagination, and are not at all real. In the same way a person can hypnotise you in a meditation into seeing light, and you will see light until the end of your life. However, this does not mean that you have reached the point of carrying light, either for yourself or for others, but only that another person has given you an illusion.

So how can we establish that what we see or hear is or is not real? That it is positive or negative? Here it is important to establish the sacred place, the private chamber, within ourselves where we can revert to just being ourselves. This means reverting to the self we create at any one time: to an archetype we are able to use, which can be changeable but must hold certain basic qualities. In this way, we will not attract the gravitational forces when we go within and we will have a central standard to which to refer. If we then raise our vibrations and listen and receive messages in which we are exhorted only to be kind, generous, good, harmless and hard-working, as opposed to creating phenomena, amassing riches or playing around with power, it is unlikely that we ourselves will have created that with which we are in touch by our own illusions. But if we start being delighted with our progress and feel that we are getting marvellous, beware! Reject whatever appears, be it guide or angel, until you are able to get to grips with it and analyse it impartially. The higher the level, the less the energy is shaped; until the highest level of all is quite formless. So long as people keep forming things into shapes, saying, 'I am this', 'I see that,' they are not being universal. Universality actually means shapelessness. Yet, for some, shape and form are vital: it would be too frightening to feel suddenly that they had no shape or place. As we go higher in evolution, shapes actually matter less rather than more. As for vision, everybody will see things slightly differently according to how advanced they are. Aside from this we are conditioned by books and preconceived notions as to how certain invisible energies manifest, and this conditioning effectively removes our ability to try to sense such things for ourselves.

Elementals

Elementals are a case in point. Many artists who depict them are more interested in designing little dresses and buttoned-up jackets than in recording the energy patterns of inter-linked etheric matter, yet the idea of interchanging energies would be a far more realistic, scientific approach to take. We know that on every plane of existence there are various types of energy interaction. Where energy gathers and the interaction is stronger something can result which is visible to the psyche. Unless we get away from our conditioning to expect definite shapes and forms, and unless we ourselves realise that we take part in shaping our impressions, we will never fully appreciate other kingdoms. Shapes are largely formed because we tend to link up with certain mental patterns and get channelled into certain pathways which have been set up as the result either of previous lives or of present conditioning; thus we always tend to experience things in particular ways.

All rays are expressed differently, and there are good and bad, or light and dark, elementals. Everything that decomposes releases energy, as does everything that is in the prime of life. All these energy patterns have evolved through the ages, through contact with other levels, and can react by shaping themselves. Sensitive photography shows leaves as having little energy globules floating beside them. A tree will form large energy globules which sometimes change their shape and form in order to gain intelligence. There are therefore spirits of the elements – earth, water, air, fire and ether – and it is for this reason that they are called elementals. We have all kinds of names for the various types of elemental: gnome, goblin, fairy, pixie, and so on. Such spirits tend to be like balls of interacting energy which can either take shape or remain as small spheres of energy and light. Sometimes it works the other way round: they remain a ball of energy and light and we form them with our senses. When we see elementals our attention often is drawn to the part of them that emits most energy, and when energies are being used in an intuitive way they tend to spiral upwards in a circle as round the head, which is why pixies, gnomes and so on are often depicted as wearing pointed caps when this is not actually the case. It is worth stating here that the elementals in a garden will gain from good vibrations in a house. Remember that elementals exist on various levels and that if we strengthen the garden we will attract the lighter ones.

Psychic contagion

Picking up signals from the environment was vital for the survival of primitive man. The second nervous system is part of what Jung calls the collective unconscious, part of the group soul system. Through this network ideas put out into the ether can be collected; often we see an epidemic of articles, books and programmes on a particular subject, all suddenly appearing at the same time. In the same way many people these days, without being aware of it, are picking up

110

the negativity of others from the atmosphere. Perhaps you go into a place, or someone comes into the room, you were feeling quite all right, but suddenly you begin to feel uneasy, depressed, a headache coming on. What happens is that you are tuning into that other person's depression, pain or block and thinking it is your own. We know that primitive man needed to sense the approach of his enemies and to find his way through the jungle and that he did these things not only through his sense of smell but through picking up vibrations with his feet. Today, in our urban civilisation this kind of sensitivity is rare; even good psychics would probably find it difficult if they were put down and had to find their way through the interior of a jungle. Nevertheless, being infected by the feelings of others is a common enough occurrence. If somebody is sitting across the room to you and you, yourself, are feeling low, you will as a rule not enjoy the highest vibrations of that other person; you will tune in on a lower note, a lower key. Becoming very open to others leads to constant upheavals – even to forms of insanity – which are due to the reawakening of sensitivity.

The faster the vibration, the quicker any thought put into the subconscious will resound. At these fast levels one is the creator of one's self. Those who are creative often respond quickly to the thoughts of others, but we have to be careful. The reawakening of this system can make us a pawn in another person's hands. Yet the slower one vibrates, the more one attracts the lower forms of nature: lower thought-forms and entities which can intensify depression and lead to disturbance.

There is another aspect too. Two people may walk into a room, one looking haggard and the other well. What may have happened is that the person who looks as if his aura needs help has just absorbed all the other's negativity. Certain individuals are like clouds in the sky, blown by the wind: nothing really affects them. But if you are the type of person who clears others, you must think seriously about your breathing and the way you relax your body. We have to remember that basically illness is caused either by wrong thinking and wrong action or by the absorption of others' negativity. There is no doubt that as we become more universal we are able to pick up others' difficulties and, on a wider scale, tune into world problems. If we possess a lot of love naturally, or can raise the force through exercises, we can help lift not only ourselves but a larger range of suffering.

Depression

Not only can we become debilitated by the moods of others, but also we may find ourselves sinking beneath depressions in the weather. One of the functions of the second nervous system was to inform human beings of changes in the elements. So if you are sitting there feeling miserable it is possible that you have become tuned in to low atmospheric pressure. Those who are depressed tend to think of themselves and then to worry because they are depressed. One way of changing this is to do something for other people: if you are busy helping others you will not have time to be depressed, you will be using up the energy that would otherwise be linking you with the depression.

Most of us are afraid of our own negativity, frightened by the idea of the devil, the force of gravity, instead of accepting it and using it constructively. We feel horrible when we have dreadful thoughts and depressions. A person will say something nasty and then sit and worry about it, stir up the darkness instead of being able to look at it. The constructive thing to do is to observe and listen to yourself. Recognise that at the point that you made that particular remark your energies may have been low. This is actually a sign from your system that you need to take another look at cleansing. We must remember that the cleaner we become the more sensitive we will be and therefore the more able to collect negative thoughts of others because we ourselves will begin to be cleansing agents. At the same time, if we reach some measure of peace and contentment we may be drawn to those who are negative and vice versa; this is a way of sharing and balancing energies.

So if you feel depressed, apply yourself constructively to the task of cleansing. First see if you have any depressing thought-forms around. Have you been thinking or saying negative things? If you have been strewing yourself and your surroundings with ugly thoughts you may need to use incense, candles, music. Consider your way of life. What pictures do you have? What books? What is the real cause of the negativity? Perhaps the whole house is impregnated and needs a spring-clean.

When you are in a very deep depression, you must use all available tools to raise yourself up. You must find someone to talk to: if you do not have friends, or a priest, or any money to pay for a therapist, you need to expel the stuff by pouring it out on to a tape, talking aloud. You need to breathe it out of your system, preferably by an open window. You need nature, good books, good music, soothing things, a lot of sleep. An animal is often a help: if you are feeling low, the presence of a small creature can raise the whole atmosphere of a house. Sometimes too much energy goes up into the roof of the mouth. It is good to put on a record, to dance and scream. If you are feeling insecure or you are doing something that calls for a bit of courage, you may find that certain insecurities well up from childhood or past lives and produce in you symptoms of depression – a general feeling of being out of sorts and unable to cope. A lot of people will actually become ill rather than do something about this. Before tackling major things it sometimes helps if you earth yourself. So if you experience this type of problem, sort yourself out. If you are quite sure you are not regurgitating your own miseries, if you have cleared out all possibilities of negativity and yet are still feeling depressed and uncomfortable, then you are going around in too open a state. You cannot afford to be unprofessional, and you must learn to close yourself down.

The pituitary gland

The pituitary, together with the pineal, is one of the main gateways into the second nervous system. It could be said that both the pineal and the pituitary are in themselves vibratory rates capable of linking up with the higher self. Both these centres act on the glands, which secrete hormones into the bloodstream. If the pituitary is inactive, this can cause problems on the physical level and it will be impossible

113

to get through to the third eye properly. It is possible to use the pituitary with a closed third eye, but it may not tune in well until the whole system comes to life; its ability to function depends on the extent to which a person can open up the whole circuit. A very clever person may be able to use these glands but not necessarily to see the invisible. He may take the energy into the third eye but focus it differently – for example, he may get amazing hunches about horses winning races.

The pituitary functions better in darkness, and it is difficult to operate the third eye in bright sunlight. We can all become more aware in darkness, and the moon itself has a definite effect on the right side of the brain; human beings generally become more open under its influence. Yet, for some, darkness and the intuitive levels it may bring seem terrifying, the great unknown. Night is a time when the body tries to heal itself. This is one of the purposes of sleep, and it calls for a change in consciousness which is sometimes hard to achieve in the case of negative, depressed individuals whose minds are inclined to whirl in circles and to become increasingly heavy as they plunge into unreasonable depths. Life nowadays moves so fast – everyone seems to be rushing to catch up with themselves – and this sleeplessness, this lying awake with a churning mind, is common and to a great extent prevents the system from clearing itself. In various stages of sleep we release unacceptable voltages. We can work out fears and clear our thought-forms, which may be reabsorbed, emerging as images on subconscious levels. Suppressed symptoms always well up in left-brained people who have been dealing with mundane things all day; at night their psyches, which need to escape, start to open. Yet for some this is impossible, for their psyches are trapped: they are unable to reach that beautiful state between sleep and wakefulness in which we have access to subconscious levels and the programming of our computer lies within our grasp. When a person is very tense he may jerk violently as his nervous system starts to release its tension and the subtle body tries to loosen itself. If we are free enough etherically, we can remove ourselves from the body altogether and travel astrally. Some people have daydreams as opposed to working out scenes by night; if part of their brain is overcharged, their minds will jump about all over the place and may produce visual images and experiences. In such cases there is a possibility that the energy is rising either up the left or right side of the spine rather than up the centre.

Dizziness

This may mean that we need to earth ourselves and be more practical. When we become dizzy we are actually moving into a state that the dervishes worked to achieve. It means that somehow we have produced enough energy to speed up the aura and change our patterns; we have become a whirl of energy.

Headaches

Some headaches are caused by the inability of certain areas to function well. If, for example, you open the third eye and then sit in meditation, gathering energy but are quite unable to open the top of the head, or if you exercise your body a great deal but fail to include the facial muscles, you will end up with permanent headaches and probably dependent on those who are able to remove the headache through some power of hypnosis. Women often suffer from headaches before their periods: a woman's vibration changes through her monthly cycle and passes through various rates. The inability of her system to cope with chemical changes often causes water retention.

One way of clearing headaches favoured by orientals is to rub the roof of the mouth in the direction of the pain; if it is on the left, for example, rub the left side of the palate; massaging it either with the tongue or the finger. This will relax the muscles and bring help to the whole area. In order to keep a large third eye open and under control we need to bring to life all the acupuncture points around the head, and we may have to raise the ears by as much as half an inch so as to be comfortable. If the roof of the mouth starts to go up causing the ears to become immobile, this will lead to enormous problems of stress. If the eyebrows start to alter their position and the top of the head is unable to move back, this also causes problems. If we frown and gather in the middle of the forehead, this, too, causes tension which may have unfortunate results.

Suggestions for improving the third eye

Think of the third eye centre as a white vibratory wing structure which spreads out behind as well as in front and on either side. The more this centre appears like a mirror, the more the person is like a reflector. Think of the moon reflected on water; think of a starlit evening – lovely silvery light. Try to feel a deep inward journey. Any tension in any area will be reflected here from past and present lives. So relaxation of the whole face helps, as does breathing well into the third eye centre itself in order to relax the forehead. Imagine a lovely blue colour in the throat, indigo in the forehead. Imagine, then, that white light is streaming down and entering the third eye, which becomes alight and sends down signals into the whole of the chakra system, streaming down through the whole body. Keep the breath steady and imagine the energy moving into all the centres. The surface of your skin is glowing. Your aura becomes bigger and bigger. Everything inside you is alive and alert. Then close up by thinking of each centre separately, and imagine each centre moving into a jewel shape; that the jewels are shining and the top of the head looks like a large, clean diamond.

Physical exercises for the face and head

The area behind the ears has a powerful effect on the third eye, and so does the area over the ears. If the ears have drooped due to the muscles here becoming slack, then any pressure experienced during the opening of the third eye will cause headaches. You may have continual pain here until you have learnt what to do with your face, your neck and the back of your head. All the muscles must be in tune.

1   Rub the hands together to fill them with energy and then put the heels of the palms close together above the eyebrows, the fingers on the top of the head. Concentrate

on this area. The idea is to contract the muscle beneath the hair which pulls the forehead up. Do this by tilting the head forward. On the in-breath lift the head and look up; if possible hold for a count of six, then drop the head down on the out-breath.

2 Take the heel of one hand and place it between the eyebrows. Press down on the in-breath and contract the eyebrows for a few minutes. Release on the out-breath. This will galvanise the muscles at the back of the head and those around the eyes.

3 Place the heels of the palms over the ears. Beneath each temple is a strong muscle that lifts the skin at the sides of the face and ears. Contract this muscle by pulling up the ears on the in-breath and holding for a few moments. Release on the out-breath.

4 Behind the ears are muscles which are responsible for pulling back the ears. Put the fingertips behind the ears, and on the in-breath pull back the ears, making them contract. Release on the out-breath.

5 Put the hands at the back of the neck where the hairline ends, fingers about an inch apart. Beneath the scalp, at the back of the head, is a sheath of muscles. Contract these by pulling the scalp towards the fingertips on the in-breath, moving the fingers towards one another. Relax by opening the fingers and stroking the neck.

6 Rub the hands together once more and place the heels of the palms around the bony structure of the eyes. Tilt the head, lift it up and back on the in-breath and look up. Hold this position for a few seconds. As you look up the first time, concentrate on the centre of the forehead, then on the beginning, centre and ends of the eyebrows respectively. When you release bring the head down, close the eyes, cup them with your hands and relax.

7 Pull the lips together as though you are about to whistle or blow a kiss. Do this a few times. Then open the mouth as wide as possible.

8 Tilt the head back. Open and shut the mouth four or five times, clenching the jaw. Then clench the lower lip over the upper lip several times.

Exercise for visualisation

Imagine you are holding a crystal in your hand and that as you look into it you see a beautiful blue lake with waterlilies floating on its surface. As you gaze, imagine that the lilies open up so that you can feel you are seeing more and more. Your gaze is expanding, so that you can see pine trees and a path winding away under the fragrant branches. As you begin to walk down the path, try to be aware of the trees on either side; and as you approach a bend in the path you can see in the distance a beautiful white building. When you are ready, go up to the door. Now watch very carefully, waiting for it to open. Go through the doorway and into a room where there are a number of people, all of them stretching and relaxing. Imagine a warm atmosphere, safe and secure; lie down here, relax and stretch.

When you have done enough, get up, walk out of the door and into the next room, where there are more people sitting very still, using their minds, trying to sense their bodies, trying to feel how they are functioning. Join them and tune into your own body; watch it closely and listen. When you have done that, imagine a person in a white robe moving through the room giving everyone an object. This can be whatever you choose: a flower, a stone, a jewel. It is there to direct the mind. As you gaze upon it quietly, try to feel its properties and you will reach a point at which you feel the contact becoming deeper so that you feel a lovely sense of affinity. The purpose of this exercise is for you to think of your object with no other thoughts whatever rising up.

When you are ready, quietly get up and walk into a third room. Here everyone is concentrating on relaxation, particularly relaxation of the heart. Sit down and relax, make sure your hands have no tension, feel the shoulders, the hips and the legs growing softer and dreamy. Feel that the body is having a really good rest. Just be peaceful and rest here. When you are ready and rested, you see a staircase. You climb the stairs and enter yet another room. Here you can learn about energies and how to direct them so that when too much energy goes into the head you can earth yourself; you can operate and control your energies so that they open and close correctly.

118

Look well, and when you have done this, walk out in search of your own room. This is a room for you alone; it has nothing to do with anyone else. It is a particular room in which you can be absolutely secure, you can be whatever you want to be. You do not have to feel shape or form; you can feel part of the universal flow. As you step in here you can feel you are no longer in any way bound to the body. Here is your room in which your higher self can manifest: feel that you can go there and you can tune into the highest aspect of yourself. You can think of this in any way you like; you can form it or not. You can think of it as a good friend who has given you his love and blessing. This aspect of you is very still, beautifully serene and encompassing all things, and you feel nothing but peace. Now, with the knowledge of this lovely companionship, take a candle, put it in a specially beautiful place you have made in this room – on an altar, in a shrine, on a table where there stands a fragrant flower – and here put the names of all those you would like to be healed and blessed. When you have done this, try to listen to what this higher aspect of yourself, this lovely friend, needs, and see whether you can draw something of this aspect into yourself. Observe what comes – just a sense of well-being is enough. When you are ready, come back into your body. If you like, you can walk back down the stairs and along the path by the trees to the lake and go back to holding your crystal. Have a good stretch when you have finished, and give your hands and feet a rub.

CHAPTER EIGHT

The Top of the Head

At the top of the head lies the pineal gland, which, like the pituitary, becomes active at night, under the influence of the moon. When you are tuned into this gland you enjoy a change of brainwave and a certain fluid is released which is said to keep you eternally young and bring you untold gifts.

Also at the top of the head are marvellous luminous energies which prevail like sheaths through all the bodies and which move in waves, crossing one another and forming different types of geometric patterns composed of all the vibrations we have acquired in our various lives. These are the vibrations of the higher self, and unless we have some way of absorbing them we will never be able to tune into them or use them. Throughout history different cultures have depicted these overhead energies in different ways: there is the golden halo of the Christian saint; the sun disc of ancient Egypt; the feathers of the Red Indian headdress; the crown, the lotus, and so on. These symbols are not just artistic appreciations but a fairly literal representation of what a sensitive person actually sees and translates into tangible form.

Angels

Just as artists have represented the heavy gravitational forces as devils, so they have portrayed the highest intuitive levels as angels.[37] These vibrations move in waves and appear to psychics as shimmering white feathers – hence the wings of angels. The Aztecs wore beautiful cloaks made of feathers to symbolise being wrapped in the highest vibrations.

The popular notion of an angel flying about like a bird is not correct: 'angel' is simply a name for a force field and the

wi'   atterns that move in waves, creating
r   selves which make them seem
                           y different kinds of angels in
                           ioms, elements, rays and dimen-
                           ates at a different rate. Some of the
                           netrate all things, but many are like
                           deed, 'fire' is a better description of
                           'angel with feathery wings'. They seem
                           mobile, full of light and love and powerful
en   annot be compared to anything we see on
earth,   you can, imagine each angelic vibration as a
kind of   nery flame, dancing, very alive, shimmering,
which through contacting the atomic structure of a room
can light up in any part of it, form an etheric body and
manifest.

A person on a level slightly higher than average might see
an angelic entity purely as a ball of energy or, if they were
experiencing it internally, might feel it as an enormous whirl
of energy. In the same way, the highest energy of all, the
Christ Consciousness, may become an external projection
outside our bodies, looking at us; or we may sense it waking
up inside us in various ways. With a person who is only
partially evolved, the angelic will in turn illuminate only
partially; the whole field will not be used, and it will become
more shaped and human since the vibration has slowed down
a little. Angels vibrate on every ray. Our own personal
guardian is available or unavailable, shaped or unshaped, its
energies change according to our own. We tend to think that
everybody has an angel trotting behind them, going onto
buses and into cars. This is not correct. Angels do not flap
their wings, fly away and come back when we need them;
they are part of an energy field which manifests itself in
different ways and can at times give you the right idea. So
what on earth, you may ask, is happening when this sheath of
energy starts to manifest and even considers speaking? Let us
suppose you have a problem and call upon your angel. Providing you raise your mind and do not lower it by grumbling
and complaining you may succeed in stimulating your chakras. Then, as your energy begins to flow you may produce
more activity in the pineal and pituitary centres and so tune

into levels whereat, it could be said, lies the answer to every prayer. We can put this another way, by saying that at the speed of light you can receive an energy which the higher self, like a wireless transmitter, can turn into words for the lower self.

Sometimes we can look like angels, sometimes like devils; for in saying that each of us has an angel we also have to say that each of us has a devil. What we have to do is become like our angels: they are there to open the doors to higher consciousness.

Reincarnation

Our aim on earth is to achieve total adaptability and control, not just of our inner energies but of our surface energies as well. It is the refining of the auric space around us that we attempt to bring about through a succession of lives. The idea is that as we reincarnate we should raise our vibratory rates so that everything we touch becomes more and more deeply infused with the spirit and we ourselves become more and more beautiful. It is for this reason that we incarnate again and again, experiencing different types of body, both male and female. The goal is to reach a state in which only the mind and spirit function and the physical is no longer necessary. For this purpose we are repeatedly drawn back to earth to learn to cope with the vibrations with which we are uneasy. We are trying to explore wavelengths we have never before touched, never before wanted to touch, so as to achieve a balance. To evolve towards the light we must deal with all rays, all vibratory rates; and once we have touched high levels part of us will be able to collect a consciousness that will help others do the same. However, if we go back to all the things we have done before instead of seeking and going beyond, we will be locked into those patterns again. Perhaps, for example, we are drawn frequently to medicine yet never turn our hand to anything artistic. Perhaps we have isolated ourselves completely from the world, worked through initiations, emptying our centres of desire, filling our lives with creativity and healing. Perhaps we have gained our knowledge and inspiration from nature, from plants and animals. Perhaps we have lived celibate lives quite removed from all physical, sexual relationships; or, perhaps again, we have had numerous such associations. Sometimes lives are devoted to relationships; sometimes to healing. When we ourselves have learnt a lesson, we are often led to dedicate our time to helping others with difficult lives; yet difficult lives may be times of reckoning in which we have to rid ourselves of excess karma. We learn to accept different people and to smooth out corners in personal make-up. We may inherit faulty bodies or bring with us other weaknesses, because perhaps we have enjoyed too much power in the past. We may have had a previous life of intense poverty, suffering and hate which has led to the traits of our present character; or we may have been very rich so that in this life we are poor. If previously we have led a bad life, there is really nothing we can do beyond physical levels to lessen the pain or save ourselves. By reincarnating we get a chance – or several chances. At least on earth we have placebos. If life gets really painful we can drink, smoke and stuff ourselves with food. We may suffer, but we can have moments of enjoyment as well.

The idea of karma is balance. It is a kind of internal banking system through which we accumulate debts and pay them back so that our accounts may eventually tally. If we see ourselves as having a great deal of negativity, we can look closely at our lives and see whether we can clear up some karmic debts. Our karma is very much linked with the sort of thoughts we strew around. If we confess our sins they will certainly be taken away, but the point is that the karma, the punishment, due for the sins remains; it can only be lifted if we do something constructive about eliminating the negativity from our system. Everything negative has to be neutralised by something positive.

Sometimes we actually need a body which is unable to express itself: this may be part of a karmic debt. Let us suppose we had a lot of power, many servants and subjects, and we abused that power. We may now need a life in which we are unable to order others around: our time may be dictated by people who may or may not be kind enough to do things for us. A person's higher self will always want to repay karma in any way it can. Those who get things for nothing will never be able to clear up their debts or balance themselves, so it is important to return energies. If you have no money to give those who help you, who perform for you some kind of service, you should either give them your energy in some way or, if this is inappropriate, help someone else. 'Help' means something that can be acted upon. We should never accept large amounts of energy in any form without becoming a more generous person in other ways.

We meet the same person in many lives, and we have to settle our karma with him eventually. We have karmic ties which we can fulfil either well or badly. We may, for instance, be karmically linked to one person in a life, yet spend all our time thinking about another. This means that not only are we failing to give the first person our full attention and thereby work out our karma properly but by wrong thoughts and actions we are probably acquiring more. The more promiscuous we are, the more trouble we shall have in the next life because of the cords we have set up, all of which will have to be worked out. One of the most vital tests for a temple dancer was a karmic screening to determine whether she was capable of renouncing the world and dedicating herself to the pursuit of fine vibrations; to see whether she could 'de-cord' herself and give up all idea of marriage and children.

Fundamentally, karma and ignorance – ignorance being the root of all suffering – go together. In other words, not to know, to be ignorant and therefore to suffer, to be unable to cope, unable to pull or get ourselves together, to be disintegrated by negativity, may be our karma. It may be the result of some debt we have accumulated in a past life, so that on this particular stretch we have to fumble our way through a fog of unknowing.

One of the many reasons for our coming to earth is to learn about ourselves, why we are here, what we are and how to develop ourselves. We select a particular type of parent, a lineage which has already developed certain brands of energy: that is, we try to ensure that we do not get a body with a lower energy pattern than we deserve. We have built up our systems over many lives, and with each incarnation we choose the chakras we need in order to fulfil a special task. The four root races all have different kinds of energy patterns and therefore different kinds of responses: one has only to observe the difference in the ways an African and an Englishman dance to realise this. Gradually, over many lives, gifts build up and vibrations become strengthened.

It is possible that if we have a lot of karma, or have burnt out our circuits, we will be born to parents with lower patterns because they too may have curtailed the size of their chakras through repeated abuse and misuse. If we have misdirected energies in a previous life we will choose a body with a reduced ability in certain chakras: perhaps we may inherit a week heart, or perhaps a chakra system in which the heart area requires cleansing. Imagine the scene as we prepare ourselves for reincarnation. 'OK,' one of your friends might say, 'I'll be your mother, because I'm coming down. I'm going into this lineage and I'm likely to turn out like So-and-so. There'll be certain stresses I may have inherited that I shall pass on for you to grow through. Perhaps I will go wrong myself – perhaps, for example, I will start to smoke so that you will be born small. That would mean I will be karmically involved with you,' and so on.

Thus we come down to earth with the intention of learning certain lessons and maintaining particular points in our lives. When cords are ready to open, the energy produces coincidences and people meet to work out their destiny together. Cords can comfort and strengthen us: if we are going through a difficult patch we may meet somebody who is corded to us, who can help us. Yet there is always a risk of certain changes taking place. Life is not a case of a group of actors learning a script and going through a performance, for free will comes in and turns the whole thing into an adventure. Let us suppose that we are meant to meet a particular person at a certain stage of our life but because we have done something stupid we have the wrong energy, the wrong vibration, and the meeting is unable to take place. In any case, it is the people to whom we are closest who represent our biggest challenge: it is our attitude to these that usually has to alter. Often we come down to earth without the person with whom we have the closest affinity, or even without anyone to support us. Sometimes the ideal companion appears later in life, when we have worked out some faults and achieved a measure of progress. Sometimes progress is slow. We may meet people with whom we work for only a time; often we feel we are unable to exist without someone who has just left us, perhaps through death or by going off with another. Yet this is not really a tragedy at all: we have probably worked out the karma between us and separated. If a certain person is holding us back, if we are corded to an individual who is stopping us from progressing, then something will happen in one life or another that will set us free.

Our lives are, in effect, journeys. Along the way we reach various crossroads. One way of knowing whether the direction we take is the right one or not is to see how things fall into place in one direction and not in another. In the course of a week we may perhaps meet ten people: one we will follow through and see again but the others we will not. This is not a case of sitting thinking about it, it is simply that there is no energy produced in the other directions. When our path is correct, the people whom we meet, with whom we work, are the by-products not of our own needs but of that which needs to be done in the light of evolution. So often we launch ourselves optimistically into projects and relationships; things that seemed sure of success fail. It is important to look closely at ourselves, at how much we contribute. If we are not getting the partner, the job, the income we would like, perhaps it is not right for us to have these things. Getting the things we want is not important: it is what we are going to do with them, how we are going to serve that matters. If we received a lot of money, for example, what would we do with it? We need to observe the patterns in our lives. It is from the recurring failures and the pain that we may get some inkling of the lessons we have set ourselves. And running away from the job by committing suicide is no answer: eventually we will be led back again to the same unresolved situation at earth level. We must therefore try to accept our lives.

Death

Contrary to most people's expectations, death should be a beautiful and liberating experience – one of the peak experiences of life. Some of us do look upon death as an adventure: for instance, Freya Stark, the intrepid explorer, looks forward to it as the ultimate in exploration. For most people, however, the idea of death contains nothing but horror: a fear of being cold and alone, probably somewhere dark and certainly completely unknown. Yet if we could think of death in the context of orgasm, as being the crowning climax of all, it might perhaps help to cast new light on the subject. It is interesting that Michael Perry, Archdeacon of Durham, draws the parallel between sex and death: 'Death is like sex used to be,' he writes. 'Everybody does it but nobody talks about it.'[38] He goes on to underline the parallel by talking about the 'pornographers of death', the 'voyeurism' (with so much death in the newspapers and on the television), the 'journalistic titillation'. In ancient Egypt, death was looked upon as an exquisite experience, and it is only fear that creates a blockage to appreciating properly the change. All those people who have nearly expired and have subsequently returned to life bring back with them the knowledge that death is nothing but a pleasant transition. These days quite a number of works are available which chart the last moments of a substantial number of individuals, all of whom have been subsequently resuscitated.[39] In America there is even an International Association for Near-Death Studies with its own newsletter and twice-yearly academic publication.[40]

Dr Thelma Moss, the well-known American parapsychologist, cites in her book,[41] which investigates scientific discoveries and explorations in the psychic world, the case of the medium Arthur Ford. While critically ill in hospital, Ford found himself floating above his bed. He could see his body lying there below, yet took no more interest in it than if it had been a cast-off piece of clothing; he was himself, but without any sense of having a body. Coming towards him were people he had known and whom he had thought of as dead. At one stage of his experience a court of higher beings considered his condition. They were seriously concerned about his dissipation of opportunity, his failure to accomplish what he had been meant to fulfil. It was made clear that he would have to return. Like a spoilt child he baulked, stiffened and fought against going. He then had a sudden sense of hurtling through space and found himself back in his hospital bed: he had apparently been in a coma for two weeks.

Dr Moss quotes another case, that of Private Ritchie.[42] Ritchie had sprung out of his hospital bed and, looking back, had seen a person lying there dead. The room began to fill with light: there was no word in the language to describe the intensity and brilliance of that light. He then saw every single episode of his life, every event, conversation and thought, as palpably as a series of pictures. Each asked a single question: 'What have you done with your life, with your time on earth?'

It is perhaps ironic that the litany in *The Alternative Service Book*[43] should extend to us the supplication, 'from violence, murder and dying unprepared, good Lord, deliver us'; ironic because, in spite of the outstanding work done in this area by such pioneering spirits as Dr Elizabeth Kubler-Ross, the majority of us arrive at the hour of our death without any preparation or instruction as what to do during and after it; indeed, the topic is one that is completely ignored by our left-brained society. Modern man may have overcome his superstition, but he has not overcome his fear of death, which lurks, a dark and unknown monster, somewhere out there beyond. Yet we cannot just leave our bodies. Something has to move in order for us to do so: the physical and the etheric must disengage themselves from each other. In the temples, ancient initiations prepared the neophytes for the whole process, rather in the way that today candidates are prepared for religious confirmation. The exercises included being drugged and fasting for long periods, until the individual became extremely weak. He would then be brought out of his body under expert instruction so that he would know there was nothing to fear, that nothing ever really died; that he was immortal. With this knowledge behind him, he would be able to work hard so that when the time came he could make the most of the supreme feeling of release, the lightness and joy that come at the moment of departure from the physical body.

Some cultures had rules and regulations laid down as to what you can expect to meet and what you must say. Some of these instructions can be found in *The Tibetan Book of the*

Dead,[44] the 'traveller's guide to other worlds', as Sir John Woodruffe called it.[45] Here the dying man is consoled and fortified by rites that continue day and night, his attention being drawn consistently to the very fact that he is dying; that death is only an initiation into another life and that he is now experiencing the Clear Light of Pure Reality. His spirit is assisted through each stage of death by conches, drums and cymbals and chants that are recited again and again into his ear so as to impress themselves upon his mind and enable his spirit to leave the body; renounce its attachment to relations and material things and find its way to other realms. The lama chants:

> O nobly-born (So-and-so by name), the time hath now come for thee to seek the Path, thy breathing is about to cease. Thy *guru* hath set thee face to face before with the Clear Light; and now thou art about to experience it in its Reality . . . wherein all things are like the void and cloudless sky, and the naked, spotless intellect is like unto a transparent vacuum without circumference or centre. At this moment, know thou thyself; and abide in that state . . . O nobly-born, that which is called death being come to thee now, resolve thus: O this now is the hour of death. By taking advantage of this death, I will so act, for the good of all sentient beings . . . by resolving in love and compassion towards this Sole Perfection . . . O nobly-born (So-and-so), listen. Now thou are experiencing the Radiance of the Clear Light of Pure Reality. Recognise it.[46]

As the actual moment of death draws near, various changes may be felt. Some people are very susceptible to the opening of their ear centres: if these open up prematurely, they may hear sounds – beautiful music, perhaps. As things speed up we may hear the inner sounds of the body, and some of us may sense a marvellous tranquillity, feel as though the body is floating on water, see crystal structures or beautiful white buildings. Others, like Private Ritchie, may see a beam of white light coming to collect them, or find their friends or other special people helping them. Overall there is a wonderful feeling of peace and, as vibrations quicken, the physical body is able to disengage itself easily. The faster the vibrations, the less the pain and fear. If, on the other hand, we are unprepared and vibrating slowly, if we have been pulled down by the forces of gravity and so remain attached to our bodies and possessions, we will fight to hold on and find it difficult to accept the transformation.

It is possible for us to help others to accept pain and death: through linking our minds with the higher self of the person in question we can act as a go-between. To do this we should gently raise our vibrations, which will ease the other person's fight for survival. It is better if there are two helpers: one to stand at the feet and the other at the head. If, however, you alone are helping to do this, place your hands over the dying person's head and link your own higher self to his.

Death, in short, can be the hour of illumination: the actual process of dying offers the greatest possibility of attaining insight and liberation. Afterwards it is likely that we will have to come to terms with ourselves and our experiences. We may have to straighten ourselves out and, like Arthur Ford, go through some kind of judgement whereby we will be counselled in order to understand our weaknesses. We must realise that there can then be no secrets: no longer will it be possible for us to hide behind skin. There will be no such things as excuses; only our energy, our vibrations, will matter. We shall be judged according to how we were and what we are, and everyone else will know precisely what we are like. The point will be this: how we have learnt our lessons and faced our sufferings, how we have mastered the forces of gravity and raised our vibrations – in other words, how light we have managed to become. We shall not be required to stand up and explain ourselves: everyone will know our mind in any case, and be able to reach right through us. Good friends may come to try and draw out the things we have done so that we may be released and recognise what we still have to do. The Egyptian and Tibetan Books of the Dead describe judgements that are in essentials so alike as to suggest a common origin. In the Tibetan version, Dharma-Raja, king and judge of the dead, corresponds to Osiris in the Egyptian version. Both books depict a symbolic weighing of souls. Before Dharma-Raja pebbles are placed on either side of a pair of scales, black ones on one side and white ones on the other; while before Osiris the heart and a feather are weighed against each other.

So the aim of life then is to achieve a fast, light vibration, and the only thing that counts, ultimately, is the degree of radiance or illumination of our subtle bodies. To put it another way, we seek to reach the angelic realms which may be ours through coming down to earth. It is to attain these realms that we come down again and again to experience the hardship and joys of earthly life.

Fairy tales are really allegories of life, of the journey towards the light, towards universality, or in other words the journey towards becoming whole through the marriage of opposites. *Snow White* and *Cinderella*, for example, are stories about the female side of the psyche: it is through being gentle and humble that these heroines find their princes, marry them and live happily ever after. In the latter, the fears and faults to be overcome are symbolised by the ugly sisters who work to keep Cinderella away from her prince and therefore from becoming whole. In life it is often not possible to achieve this union of opposites. Yet at the hour of death, with nothing to hold on to, the male and female energies within us may become as one. Death can therefore be a marriage. If we raise our vibrations, it is possible for us to bridge the gap to eternal peace. When male and female qualities are finally balanced within us, we are complete.

We can end by saying that coming to earth is like going to school: when the term is over we go home, for it is holiday time – time to relax, to rest and recuperate until next term. This world is not a paradise; it is the experiences we have in it that will take us to paradise. Heaven has to begin inside ourselves. Paradise is within us, just as the future is here in the present. We can change the future by changing ourselves. We must realise that we are creating the future at this very moment: if at this moment we are able to see ourselves in a clear light, we can, in the words of the fairy tale, live happily ever after.

Notes and References

Preface

1 For more information on Kundalini, see Lee Saunella, *Psychosis or Transcendence* (San Francisco: H. S. Dakin, 1976).
2 Sergei Bertenson and Jay Leyda, *Sergei Rachmaninoff* (New York: New York University Press, 1956).

Introduction

3 C. G. Jung, Foreword to *Man and His Symbols* (London: Granada, 1982).
4 Ibid.
5 Lilla Bek and Annie Wilson, *What Colour Are You?* (Wellingborough: Turnstone, 1981).

Chapter One

6 Henry Gris and William Dick, *The New Soviet Psychic Discoveries* (London: Sphere Books, 1979).
7 For further information on the energies of stones, see *New Scientist*, 21 October 1982, pp. 166–71, 'The Dragon Project'; *New Scientist*, 1 September 1983, p. 627, 'Bringing UFO's Down to Earth'; Paul Devereux, *Earth Lights* (Wellingborough: Turnstone Press, 1982).
8 For further information on this aspect of life in ancient Egypt, see R. A. Schwaller de Lubicz, *The Temple in Man* (New York: Autumn Press, 1978); and Isha Schwaller de Lubicz, *The Opening of the Way* (New York: Luner Traditions International, 1982).
9 Tertullian, *On The Soul*, quoted in J. Stevenson (ed.), *A New Eusebius* (London: SPCK, 1957).
10 Ibid.
11 Elaine Pagels, *The Gnostic Gospels* (London: Weidenfeld & Nicolson, 1980).
12 Joseph Head and S. L. Cranston, *Reincarnation in World Thought* (New York: Julian Press, 1977).
13 Ibid.
14 D. Milner and E. Smart, *The Loom of Creation* (New York: Harper & Row, 1976).
15 Ibid.
16 Laurens Van Der Post, *The Lost World of the Kalahari* (Harmondsworth: Penguin, 1964); *A Story Like the Wind* (Harmondsworth:

Penguin, 1974); *A Far-Off Place* (Harmondsworth: Penguin, 1976).
17 Roger Dalet, *Relief from Pain with Finger Massage*, trans. L. Zuch (London: Hutchinson, 1979).
18 Jonathan Cott, *Stockhausen: Conversations with the Composer* (London: Picador, 1974).
19 Fritjof Capra, *The Tao of Physics* (London: Wildwood House, 1975).
20 Ibid.
21 *The Dialogue of the Saviour* (see Elaine Pagels, *Gnostic Gospels*).
22 Capra, *Tao of Physics*.
23 Milner and Smart, *Loom of Creation*.
24 Philippa Pullar, *The Shortest Journey* (London: Unwin Paperbacks, 1984).
25 Gris and Dick, *New Soviet Psychic Discoveries*.
26 Ibid.

Chapter Two

27 I. Schwaller de Lubicz, *The Opening of the Way*.
28 Ibid.
29 Frank Barr, *Brain/Mind Bulletin*, 11 July and August 1983.

Chapter Three

30 Gris and Dick, *New Soviet Psychic Discoveries*.

Chapter Four

31 See *The Most Holy Trinosophia of The Comte de Saint-Germain*, with an Introduction by Manly P. Hall (Los Angeles: Philosophical Research Society, 1962).
32 Ibid.
33 Ibid.

Chapter Five

34 Thelma Moss, *The Probability of the Impossible* (London: Granada, Paladin Books, 1979); Gris and Dick, *New Soviet Psychic Discoveries*.

Chapter Six

35 R. A. Schwaller de Lubicz, *The Temple in Man,* and I. Schwaller de Lubicz, *The Opening of the Way*.
36 Pagels, *The Gnostic Gospels*.

37   See Peter Lamborn Wilson, *Angels* (London: Thames and Hudson, 1980) for examples of angels from every century and tradition.

38   Michael Perry, *Psychic Studies* (Wellingborough: The Aquarian Press, 1984).

39   Karlis Osis and Erlendur Haraldsson, *At the Hour of Death* (New York: Avon Books, 1977); Michael A. Simpson, *The Facts of Death* (Englewood Cliffs, NJ: Prentice-Hall International, 1979); Raymond Moody, *Life After Life* (Atlanta, Georgia: Mockingbird Books, 1975); J. C. Hampe, *To Die is Gain: The Experience of One's Own Death* (London: Darton, Longman and Todd, 1979); Elizabeth Kubler Ross, *On Death and Dying* (London: Tavistock Publications, 1970).

40   The latter is entitled *Anabiosis*.

41   Moss, *The Probability of the Impossible*. Dr Moss draws her information from Arthur Ford's book, *Unknown but Known* (London: Thames and Hudson, 1980).

42   George Ritchie with Elizabeth Sherrill, *Return from Tomorrow* (Eastbourne, Sussex: Kingsway, 1978).

43   *The Alternative Service Book*, 1980.

44   Chogyam Trungpa and Francesca Fremantle, *The Tibetan Book of the Dead* (Berkley, Calif: Shambala, 1975).

45   Sir John Woodruffe's Introduction to *The Tibetan Book of the Dead* (Oxford: Oxford University Press, 1960).

46   *The Tibetan Book of the Dead*.